THE
BETRAYAL
OF AMERICA

THE
BETRAYAL
— OF —
AMERICA

How the Supreme Court
Undermined the Constitution
and Chose our President

VINCENT BUGLIOSI

FOREWORDS BY
MOLLY IVINS AND GERRY SPENCE

Thunder's Mouth Press / Nation Books
New York

Published by
Thunder's Mouth Press/Nation Books
An Imprint of Avalon Publishing Group Incorporated
841 Broadway, Fourth Floor
New York, NY 10003

Nation Books is a co-publishing venture of the Nation Institute and
Avalon Publishing Group, Incorporated.

Library of Congress Control Number: 2001089202

ISBN 1-56025-355-X
9 8 7 6 5 4 3 2 1

Designed by Pauline Neuwirth
Printed in the United States of America
Distributed by Publishers Group West

CONTENTS

THE
BETRAYAL
OF AMERICA

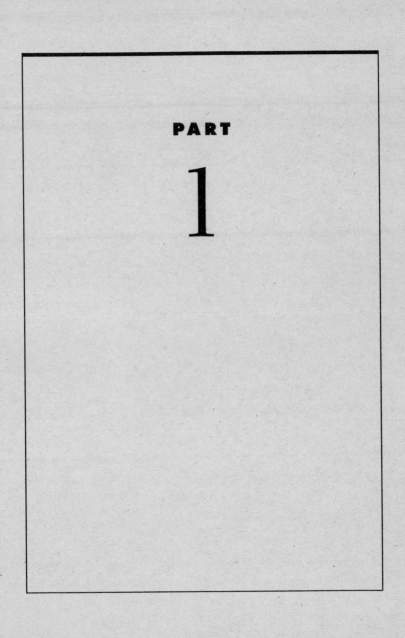

PART

1

PREFACE

by

THE EDITORS OF *THE NATION*

IN THE COURSE of American history the nation has been confronted with wrongful events that went to the core of its existence, and the resolution of those events spoke of who we are as a people. Beyond question, the U.S. Supreme Court's handing the office of the presidency to George W. Bush by its ruling on December 12, 2000, was one of them. And with these epochal events there have been Americans who have stood up and spoken out against these wrongs: for example, Tom Paine against British control of the colonies; Edward R. Murrow against the vicious and false charges made by Joseph McCarthy; Daniel Ellsberg leaking the Pentagon Papers to the *New York Times*. With his article in the February 5, 2001, *Nation* magazine titled "None Dare Call It Treason," Vincent Bugliosi takes his place in this special pantheon of patriots with his powerful, brilliant, and courageous exposé of crime by the highest court in the land. Readers' response to the article drew the largest outpouring of letters and e-mail in the magazine's 136-year history. Bugliosi's brave and devastating refutation of the Supreme Court's decision in *Bush v. Gore*, halting a recount in Florida and awarding the election to Bush, tapped a deep reservoir of outrage among our readers.

Here are a few samples:

"[Bugliosi's article] gave me heart that I am not alone in my outrage."

"Vincent Bugliosi has made me angry all over again—and I'm happy he did."

"One of the most important articles I've ever seen, up there with the Pentagon Papers."

"Should be read by every American."

"One of the most intelligent, bold, and straightforward articles I have ever read."

"Bravo, bravo. Now can any one of us DO something about it."

". . . the most important document to come out of the entire farce called an election."

"How fitting it is that the lowest point in the history of our Supreme Court is the subject of the best article I've ever read in *The Nation*."

"Thank god for Vincent Bugliosi. A voice crying out what needs to be heard."

"I cannot express my elation at finding this article."

An internal e-mail from *The Nation* copy editor Judith Long to editor Katrina vanden Heuvel on January 21 says it all: "Katrina, we're getting so much mail on the Bugliosi piece that I fear my computer is going to melt!! People are enraged and want to know what to do."

In impassioned yet impeccably reasoned prose, Bugliosi shows that what the five conservative Justices on the Supreme Court did, though not treason in the strictly legal sense, represented a betrayal of trust by an institution revered by Americans like no other, one that was supposed to be above the fray, above politics. As one reader put it: "It's because I DO respect the sanctity of the Court. It's because I DO hold the institution in such high regard that I want to scream out TREASON."

In the days after the Court's decision, the people who disagreed with it were hard-pressed to find in the mainstream media a passion commensurate with the distress and sense of betrayal they felt. As Bugliosi writes, too many of the press, the punditry, and the legal establishment simply paid obeisance to the prestige of the Court. Their passive acquiescence accorded legitimacy to Bush's accession.

Against this consensus, "None Dare Call It Treason" raised a bold cry of dissent in the noble tradition of public pamphleteering. Such passion as Bugliosi's is rare in an age of homogenized journalism and know-nothing television talk shows. Bugliosi harks back to a time when words and reasoned discourse were weapons to be mobilized in a great national debate.

As Election 2000 recedes into historical memory, it is imperative that "None Dare Call It Treason" be preserved in book form for future generations where it will provide a window on a contentious time and serve as a reminder of how democracy's central function of letting every citizen express his or her choice in the voting booth went awry. At our request, Bugliosi, who was in the middle of a deadline for his two-volume tome on the assassination of President Kennedy, agreed to expand on the article with a lengthy introduction, support material, amplifications, endnotes, and the relevant citations from the Supreme Court opinions and documents to bolster his case. Molly Ivins and Gerry Spence weigh in as well with their insights into the event.

We hope that as a book, Bugliosi's dissent will in the months ahead alert a wider audience to the dangerous precedent set by *Bush v. Gore*. As one of our readers wrote: "I've never felt so disenfranchised in my life." Bugliosi's words can help mobilize the forces of protest so that such an injustice never happens again.

—The Editors of *The Nation*

FOREWORD

by
MOLLY IVINS

VINCENT BUGLIOSI HAS written the modern equivalent of "J'Accuse," the famous indictment by the French journalist Émile Zola of his government's misconduct in the Dreyfus affair. The most startling thing these two historic accusations have in common is their self-evidence. You pretty much have to be a total moron to miss the reeking injustice in either case.

Bugliosi, the California prosecutor famous for putting away such baddies as Charlie Manson, is not your knee-jerk anti-government, anti-establishment citizen. His chances of being named Sweetheart of the Year by the American Civil Liberties Union are damn slim. Which makes it all the more startling that he, of all the distinguished members of the American bar who might do so, has chosen to accuse the 5–4 majority of the U.S. Supreme Court in the case of *Bush v. Gore* of criminal conduct bordering on treason.

If there were a way to emit a wolf whistle in print, I'd do it.

I am not a lawyer, but I do know that when Bugliosi quotes a Yale law professor as saying the day of the *Bush v.*

Gore decision was "like the day of the Kennedy assassination" for him and many of his colleagues, this is not an exaggeration. Old friends of mine who have been fighting for justice in this country since the time of the civil rights movement were devastated by the decision. They truly did not believe the court was capable of such a naked, shameless, political decision. As Bugliosi says, it was a "judicial coup d'état."

My own experience of the 36-Day War that followed the 2000 presidential election had nothing to do with the legal system. I'm a political reporter by trade and the day after the election I was holding up my hand like the smartest kid in class saying, "I know what chads are!" If you cover politics in Texas, you know how to cover a contested election. They happen every cycle. There is nothing mysterious or exotic about a stuck election: you recount by hand because it is the most accurate way to count. The problems with punch-card ballots are familiar. The damn things lose about three percent of the vote, so whenever it's close, you have to hand recount. Republicans do it, Democrats do it: Karl Rove, Bush's leading campaign strategist, once demanded a hand count.

As far as political reporters were concerned, everything was going along normally, except the stakes in this hung-up election were so amazing, until the U.S. Supreme Court stepped in. Since elections are conducted under state law, I never heard of a contested election that wasn't decided by the state courts.

I should note here that Texas does have statewide standards for hand recounts. Our law was passed in 1997 at the behest of Tony Garza, the very Republican secretary of state appointed by Governor George W. Bush, who signed the bill himself. In Texas we count hanging chads, swinging chads, dimpled chads, pregnant chads—in other words, any chad where it's clear how the voter meant to vote.

Here's the deal. Under the ballots in the punch-card machines is something called a chad tray, a shallow, plastic dish, about 1/4 inch deep. Here's the unfortunate thing about chads: they clump. People punch through their ballots and the chads in the tray build up into a tiny chad mountain, making it increasingly difficult for later voters to punch through the ballot. Furthermore, the rickety little tables on which these punch-card ballots are placed are so cheesy they're often out of balance, leaning to either the front or the back. Consequently, you regularly get problems either with your U.S. Senate race or Constable, Precinct Three. I have known cases where election officials forgot to clean out the chad trays before a new election, so they were full of old chads from the last bond issue, causing no end of confusion.

Now I could go on telling old tales of contested elections, but suffice it to say that I was Ms. Not-My-First-Rodeo during the 36-day war. I understood everything except the U.S. Supreme Court. Never understood what they were doing in the deal in the first place, and could not fathom why they decided what they did after that. I'm relieved to know from Bugliosi's brief that their actions were just as peculiar as they seemed.

I spent much of that time in Tallahassee, at the aptly named Ramada Limited, enjoying the fine dining at the Krispy-Kreme doughnut establishment. One forgets about small Southern cities like Tallahassee between visits. All middle-class social life takes place in private clubs. The night Al Gore conceded, there was a victory celebration at one such club near the capitol. Visiting congressional staffers (who proudly called themselves "the Republican thugs"), third-rank Bush lawyers, and prominent local republicans were gathered in a large room with several TV sets. When Gore began to speak, they hooted and jeered and taunted. The only black people in the room were wearing white coats and serving drinks off silver trays. They also had tears running down their faces, but in the curious way white people have of not looking directly at those who serve them, no one noticed.

FOREWORD

by
GERRY SPENCE

THE PRACTICE OF law is the practice of a religion, and lawyers and judges, like priests and popes, are deeply religious. As in all religions the law pronounces its dogma, determines who shall be saved and who condemned, and proclaims its own codes of conduct for its faithful to blindly follow. Like the church, the law claims ultimate authority, pursues ultimate power, and becomes Power itself. It is by the naked exercise of power that it ensures that Power shall remain in power, little of which has much to do with justice or truth or even simple logic itself.

Like true believers who bow to the claims of religious infallibility, we in the priesthood of the law have taken our own vows—one, a peculiar vow of silence. Although we are permitted to politely and "with all due respect" quietly disagree with a judge, under the severest of penalties we must never exhibit public disrespect for one. As with the church, any attack on the hierarchy of power is adjudged as heresy and is often punishable by death. Images of the miscreant in the Dark Ages burning at the stake or being stretched in two on the rack come readily to mind. Today, for any lawyer who dares attack the judiciary harshly and publicly, the punishment may be professional death.

My father used to say the line between bravery and foolery is narrow. Few have walked along that dangerous precipice with as much steadfast and principled mettle as Vince Bugliosi, a member of the legal brotherhood. To even consider privately whether the acts of those five U.S. Supreme Court Justices are criminal extends beyond the pale. But as the self-appointed prosecutor for the American public, that Brother Bugliosi should charge those judges publicly—and in clear, legible print—of criminal acts is an apostasy that steals the breath. But Brother Vincent went further. He undertook in understandable English to expose how those five high judges, simply because they had the power to do so, stole an election from the people and delivered it as the spoils of power to the new king, thereby violating the laws the Justices swore to uphold and thereby reducing themselves to common thugs. Such an act of courage is difficult for most members of this often timid profession to fully appreciate. That there is one among us who has the courage to speak the truth into the very faces of judges who purport to discover and preserve the truth is not only refreshing, it is divine.

Bugliosi has ripped the robes from those five judges to reveal the awesome obscenity beneath. He permits us to view the ghastly sight—the nude, unabashed, mostly white-skinned majority arrogantly standing above us with their legs uncrossed and their heads unturned in shame. It is a pathetic spectacle that Bugliosi beckons us to behold—this high, hallowed court and its revered majority sold out to Power. It is not so much whether he is right as that a lawyer of courage has finally dragged these judges into the light so that we, in turn, may judge them and come to our own conclusions—if, indeed, we have the courage to do so.

PART

2

PART

2

INTRODUCTION

by
VINCENT BUGLIOSI

AT THE TIME I am submitting this manuscript for publication (March 9, 2001), news organizations have not yet completed their count of all the Florida undervotes to determine who *really* won Florida's twenty-five electoral votes, and hence, the office of the Presidency of the United States. But lest anyone believe that their findings, whatever they turn out to be, are relevant in any way at all to what you are about to read, let me assure you that they are not. As I say in my *Nation* article of February 5, and it bears repeating: "It misses the point to argue that the five Justices stole the election only if it turns out that Gore overcame Bush's lead in the undervote recount. We're talking about the moral and ethical culpability of these Justices, and when you do that, the bell was rung at the moment they engaged in their conduct. What happened thereafter cannot unring the bell and is therefore irrelevant."

One thing is for sure. Irrespective of the result reached by the newspapers, we know that more Floridians *intended* to vote for Al Gore than George Bush on November 7, 2000. The confusing butterfly ballot in Palm Beach county resulted in literally thousands of people erroneously voting either for Pat Buchanan, or Al Gore and Pat Buchanan (the latter situation, called an "overvote," rendered their ballot invalid). Absent this confusion, Gore would easily have won Florida and there wouldn't have been any Supreme Court decision in *Bush v. Gore* for us to be talking about.

But apart from that, no one, not even the rabid right-wing of the Republican Party, would quarrel with the proposition that if, for example, a person premeditated the murder of a fellow human being by blowing him up in his car, but for whatever reason the explosive did not detonate, that person is unquestionably just as evil and blackhearted as he would be if his mission had not failed.

Not even God can change the past, so regardless of the findings of the newspapers, the conduct of the five conservative justices of the Supreme Court in *Bush v. Gore* remains the same. That conduct was either criminal or it was not. And if it was, a subsequent finding that Bush won the Florida vote cannot diminish, even one iota, the criminality of their act.

If Bush ends up winning, the automatic response by the mental midgets on the far right will be that the five justices acted completely properly, but even if they didn't, "It doesn't matter. Bush won the election anyway." But it is they, not those of us who are interested in justice and fair play, whose folly should be treated so dismissively.

To elaborate further on the possible results of the counting of votes in Florida by the major newspapers, if Gore ends up overcoming Bush, then Bush instantly becomes the most famous imposter in the history of democracy, one who is running this country only because of the high crime committed by the Supreme Court, and for no other reason—certainly a first in U.S. history and, I daresay, perhaps the first time that such an event has ever occurred in any duly constituted democracy.

But even if Bush ends up winning, not only does the enormity of the Court's crime, as indicated, remain identical, *but further*, the fact remains that on December 12, in direct defiance of the Constitution they swore to uphold, and without any authority at all, the Supreme Court *chose* Bush to be the next President of the United States. *At the point in time* of Bush's inauguration on January 20, his ascension to the presidency resulted not from a finding that he had won Florida after a count of all the undervotes, but simply because of the Supreme Court's decision on December 12. After all, no one has suggested that the five Justices who chose Bush to be President were clairvoyant. They had no more way of knowing how a counting of all the Florida undervotes would turn out than Madonna would.

WITH THE WIDESPREAD circulation of *The Nation* article, the catalyst for this new volume, came an unwelcome confirmation of something I had already concluded about the vast majority (not all) of human beings. They simply do not have sufficient character to rise above their own self-interest. Inasmuch as the decision of the United States Supreme Court in the case of *Bush v. Gore*, which handed the election to Bush, is irreversible, and nothing that any of us do can change this reality, I would ask you, the reader, to indulge me the idle rumination that follows.

I consider myself a moderate, one who has both liberal and conservative friends and acquaintances. If one accepts the harsh conclusions in the article you are about to read, I believe that amidst the welter of emotions it should induce is an overriding one—that of considerable anger against the five conservative Supreme Court Justices who stole the last presidential election. And indeed, almost without exception, this has been the precise response I have gotten from my liberal friends and most of my moderate ones. They want to hang these Justices in the town square at noontime.[1]

---

[1] All numbers refer to Notes beginning on p.31.

But with my conservative friends, though unable to cir-
cumvent the evidence or pierce the logic set forth in the
article (obviously, for the very few who thought they could,
and disagreed with my conclusions, what follows in this
discussion would not be applicable), and though many
have even been very complimentary about it, using adjec-
tives like "powerful," "thought-provoking," a few have even
said "great," I am still waiting (will I have to wait, as they
say, "until the cows come home"?) for my first conservative
friend or even acquaintance to show the slightest bit of
anger over what these justices did. If the reader can't deci-
pher the implications of what I have just said, I'll spell it
out for you. Their guy, Bush, got in, and they don't give a
damn how he got there. In other words, they aren't troubled in the least that the Supreme Court may have committed one of the biggest crimes in American history. Their
hatred for the Democratic Party (even though it had just
delivered, or at least contributed to the deliverance of eight
years of unprecedented prosperity and peace, and their
candidate, Bush, had no national or international experience, had no intellectual curiosity and seemed to be proud
of it, and looked as presidential as the guy who walks on
stage when the magician asks for volunteers) was such that
as long as they got those dreaded Democrats out of 1600
Pennsylvania Avenue, it was immaterial how they did it or
who their candidate was. One is reminded of Jack Ruby's
remark after killing Lee Harvey Oswald: "*Someone* had to
kill that son of a bitch."

It wouldn't be so alarming to me if this posture were only
being taken by the far right—you know, the thin-lipped,
chinless people with beady eyes of no particular color
who wear their patriotism on their sleeves, with very little
left inside. But these are regular, normal, conservative
Republicans. Why this deep-seated, almost atavistic hatred

for Democrats I really don't know.* And this blind rancor
has been going on for decades. One of Franklin D.
Roosevelt's favorite stories he used to tell during his presidency was about a wealthy businessman commuter from
heavily Republican Westchester County in New York who
would hand the newsboy at the train station a dime every
morning for the New York Times, glance at the front page,
then hand the paper back as he rushed out the door to
catch his train. Finally one day, the newsboy, unable to control his curiosity any longer, asked the man why he always
only looked at the front page. "I'm interested in an obituary
notice," the man said. "But the obituaries are on the back
pages of the paper, and you never look at them," the newsboy

---

*Personally, I have no animus for Democrats or Republicans. But my con-
tempt for the right-wing of the Republican party has no boundaries. The right wing
of the Republican Party, of course, is the group that always likes to loudly proclaim
its patriotism. But if they had a patriotic bone in their body, which they do not,
then, for example, they would want the president of the United States, even
though he's a Democrat, to do well. Why? Because if the president does well, the
entire country does well. But they only want the country to do well if one of their
own people is in office. If not, they'll do everything to destroy the president,
whether he's Clinton or any other Democrat.

Mind you, I always make a distinction between the extreme right wing and a
true conservative like the late Barry Goldwater, whom I always liked and respected. In fact, a few years before he died he told the right wing, "Do not associate my
name with anything you do. You are extremists, and you've hurt the Republican
Party much more than the Democrats have." A true conservative is one who cares
deeply about his country. Someone like John McCain, who, when the allegations
against President Clinton on the Lewinsky matter first started flying, said: "I hope
and pray that these charges are not true." In contrast, the right-wing fanatics were
hoping and praying that the charges were not only true, but that the president
would be humiliated in the eyes of the entire world, even though it would be to
the detriment of the country.

I should add that those whom I find particularly nauseating and disgusting are
the many liberals in the media who cater to the far right—and therefore, aid and
abet their cause—while quietly detesting them. These physiological marvels are
somehow able to sit and stand erect in front of a camera without a spine.

retorted. "Son," the man said, "the son of a bitch I'm interested in will be on page one."

What is disturbing to me about these conservative friends
and acquaintances of mine who aren't troubled in the least
by the fact that five Supreme Court Justices stole the election from Al Gore and his party is what it says about who,
deep down, they really are, and what their values and sense
of right and wrong truly are. If one is wondering if, in the
event the shoe were on the other foot, Democrats would be
responding the same way, my answer is that I believe they
would, though not to such a great degree. My assessment (at
least as to those on the margins of both parties) is that
although there is fanaticism among both groups, it is greater
on the far right than the far left, and the far right unquestionably is much more mean-spirited. And, of course, we
know from poll after poll that Republicans are more unlikely
to cross over to the Democratic side for any candidate or
issue than Democrats are to the Republican side.

With respect to this matter of conservative Republicans
being more than willing to overlook whatever the Supreme
Court or anyone else did to get their man in the oval office,
can you imagine if this insanity prevailed in other areas of our
society? You know, a Republican prosecutor not wanting to
prosecute Republican defendants, and Democratic prosecutors giving a free ride to Democratic defendants? Of course,
the notion is preposterous on its face, but how, I ask you, does
it differ in its essence from the fact that no Republican I have
yet met (undoubtedly, there *are* some out there) having the
slightest bit of anger over what the Supreme Court did?

Looking at the same issue but from a different perspec-
tive, a liberal female acquaintance of mine who erroneously
made the assumption that I was a conservative because of
my law enforcement background, called to congratulate me
upon reading the *The Nation* article, then added, "I didn't

know you were a liberal." The translation for this remark and the position my Republican friends and acquaintances take? If a Republican does something wrong, no Republican is supposed to criticize him (remember Ronald Regan's infantile eleventh commandment—thou shalt not speak ill of a fellow Republican), only liberal Democrats. How ludicrous can people get? I mean, objectivity is still a virtue in this country, is it not? And if it is, then in determining the culpability, or lack thereof, of the five Justices' conduct, what in the world does their political affiliation, or ours, have to do with it? I feel silly for even having to pose the question.

If any reader wants to know, let me say that if a five-member majority of the Supreme Court had done for Gore what it did for Bush, I can give you a one hundred percent guarantee I'd be writing the same, identical article you are about to read. If I may say so myself, my credibility on matters such as this is unassailable. For instance, I was strongly opposed to the destruction of the Nixon presidency over Watergate. Though I didn't condone President Nixon's conduct, I took the prevalent European view at the time of the scandal that a mature nation realistically balances the harm to the nation from the collapse of a presidency against the extent of malfeasance of the administration in power. And with Watergate, I became so upset and angry with people treating the matter as though it was so much more serious than it really was (prosecutor Leon Jaworski, incredibly, analogized it to the Third Reich, which resulted, as we know, in fifty million deaths during World War II, including the six million Jews murdered during the Holocaust), and with politicians (who, if the truth be told, virtually all try to cover up their own misconduct—and here, Nixon didn't even have any foreknowledge of the break-in) reacting with phony horror over the president's transgressions (e.g., Senator Ted Kennedy, who did everything within his power to suppress the facts of Chappaquiddick) that I actually wrote a twenty-page treatment for a book that I tentatively titled *Watergate, America's Finest Hour of Hypocrisy*, but prior commitments prevented me from following through on the book. Little could I have known that a quarter of a century later, the nation's and the media's certifiable insanity in making a Himalayan mountain out of President's Clinton's silly little girlfriend scandal, which was much less serious than Watergate, would make the response to Watergate look like a perfectly normal one.

There are two points the reader should keep in mind while reading the *The Nation* article. Although the Florida election dispute spawned a considerable number of lawsuits in the lower courts, apart from a few tangential references to them, *The Nation* article deals only with the Supreme Court decision of *Bush v. Gore* on December 12, 2000. Although Bush partisans have inevitably wanted to discuss alleged improprieties by the Florida Supreme Court, even if we assume the allegations to be true, they have nothing to do with the Supreme Court decision that handed the election to Bush— which was based solely on a purported violation of the equal protection clause of the Fourteenth Amendment—and therefore, are essentially irrelevant. If anyone doubts what I am saying, let me quote the applicable paragraph near the beginning of the opinion of the court in *Bush v Gore*:

"The petition [of George W. Bush] presents the following questions: whether the Florida Supreme Court established new standards for resolving Presidential election contests, thereby violating Art. II, Sec. 1, cl. 2, of the United States Constitution and failing to comply with 3 U.S.C. Sec. 5, and whether the use of standardless manual recounts violates the Equal Protection and Due Process Clauses. With respect to the equal protection question, we find a violation of the Equal Protection Clause." Hence, though not conclusive, if there is any inference to be drawn at all, it would have to be that the Court, in its *per curiam*, majority ruling, did *not* find that the Florida Supreme Court violated Art. II, Sec.1, cl.2 or Title 3 of the U.S. Code, Sec.5. Nothing is more common than for an appellate court, including the United States Supreme Court, to give several bases for its ruling. In fact, the majority of decisions by appellate courts contain multiple reasons for the court's decision (e.g., "in addition," "moreover," "there is a second, independent basis for _____") to bolster its validity and insulate it from subsequent attack or reversal. In *Bush v. Gore*, the Court clearly knew that its Equal Protection Clause argument was a legal gimmick. But as bad as it was, the Court must have felt it was markedly superior to the Bush argument that the Florida Supreme Court had violated Article II and Title 3, that the latter argument was too much of an embarrassment, even for them, to reduce to parchment. If not, what other possible reason could there be for the Court, knowing it was making perhaps the most important ruling in its history, not to try to fortify and buttress its ruling with these other arguments in its *per curiam* majority ruling?

Secondly, if any reader is seriously interested in learning what happened in the Supreme Court decision of *Bush v. Gore*, they have to disabuse themselves of any preconceived notion that because the Justices are wearing robes and are on the Supreme Court, the highest court in the land, they are simply incapable of conducting themselves in a manner that smacks of criminality. Because if one takes that position, a position that has no foundation in logic, he or she obviously will not be receptive to the evidence or to the common sense inferences from that evidence.

A word about judges. The American people have an understandably negative view of politicians, public opinion polls show, and an equally negative view of lawyers.[2] Conventional logic would seem to dictate that since a judge is normally both a politician and a lawyer, people would have an opinion of them lower than a grasshopper's belly. But on the contrary, the mere investiture of a twenty-five-dollar black cotton robe elevates the denigrated lawyer-politician to a position of considerable honor and respect in our society, as if the garment itself miraculously imbues the person with qualities not previously possessed. As an example, judges have, for the most part, remained off-limits to the creators of popular entertainment, being depicted on screens large and small as learned men and women of stature and solemnity as impartial as sunlight. This depiction ignores reality.

As to the political aspect of judges, the appointment of judgeships by governors (or the president in federal courts) has always been part and parcel of the political spoils or patronage system. For example, 97 percent of President Reagan's appointments to the federal bench were Republicans. Thus, in the overwhelming majority of cases there is an umbilical cord between the appointment and politics. Either the appointee has personally labored long and hard in the political vineyards, or he is a favored friend of one who has (oftentimes a generous financial supporter of the party in power). As Roy Mersky, professor at the University of Texas Law School, says: "To be appointed a judge, *to a great extent* is a result of one's political activity."

Incredibly, and unfortunately, the political connection holds true all the way up to the United States Supreme Court, where, for instance, the last three Chief Justices, like so many of their predecessors in history, have all been creatures of politics. Earl Warren, a former California Governor and Attorney General, was the chairman and keynote speaker at the Republican National Convention in 1944 and the vice-presidential nominee on the Republican national ticket in 1948. Warren Burger in 1948 was the floor manager for Minnesota Governor Harold Stassen's home-state candidacy at the Republican National Convention, and in 1952 he pledged the Minnesota delegation to Dwight D. Eisenhower's successful presidential bid at the convention. (With no previous judicial experience at all, in 1956 Burger was appointed by Eisenhower to the U.S. Court of Appeals.) Talk about the political vineyards, the current Chief Justice, William Rehnquist, who actively campaigned for Barry Goldwater in the latter's 1964 bid for the presidency, provided on-site legal advice in 1962 to Republicans assigned the task of challenging voters' credentials at a Phoenix polling station. The charge by four witnesses testifying under oath at Rehnquist's 1986 confirmation hearings for Chief Justice that Rehnquist had intimidated black and Hispanic voters on the ground of their inability to read was denied by Rehnquist.

What about Rehnquist's brethren on the current Supreme Court? In addition to their legal achievements, most have either been deeply involved in politics themselves, like Rehnquist, or worked for politicians or political administrations in Washington, D.C. For instance, Clarence Thomas was a legislative assistant to Republican Senator John Danforth of Missouri. Danforth ended up sponsoring Thomas's nomination to the Supreme Court and shepherded Thomas through the thicket of the entire nomination process. Thomas's appointment to the Court in 1991 was one of the most markedly political in recent memory. Though he was only forty-two, had never distinguished himself in any way whatsoever as a lawyer or on the bench (just one year on the U.S. Court of Appeals), and was not rated "highly qualified" by the American Bar Association, he apparently was what President George Bush was looking for at the time—a very conservative black. Remarkably, during his Senate confirmation hearings Thomas testified that he had never once debated with anyone the merits of *Roe v. Wade*, the landmark Supreme Court decision on abortion.

He has since more than lived up to his meager reputation, becoming a dutiful mynah bird, without his own independent voice, of Justice Antonin Scalia.

Justice Sandra Day O'Connor not only served three terms in the Arizona State Senate—at one point being the Arizona senate majority leader—but was a co-chairperson of the Arizona state committee to elect Richard Nixon president. Her biographer, Judith Bentley, writes in "Justice Sandra Day O'Connor" that O'Connor was very active in Republican politics in Phoenix, starting out as a county precinct worker in 1960 and in 1964 becoming the vice-chairman of the Maricopa County Republican Committee. Bentley writes (Page 49) that O'Connor "was rewarded for her years of party work" by being appointed a state senator. (She successfully ran for reelection twice.) Justice David Souter was the Attorney General of New Hampshire. Justice Stephen Breyer was chief counsel to the Senate Judiciary Committee in the Carter administration. Justice John Paul Stevens was a counsel for a House of Representatives subcommittee in the Truman administration. Justice Antonin Scalia was a lawyer in the Nixon and Ford administrations.

Since the *The Nation* article's publication, the belief in the legal community has been that Justice Anthony Kennedy was the primary author of the Supreme Court's decision giving the election to George Bush. If for no other reason, let's take a longer look at Kennedy. A November 23, 1987, article by Aaron Freiwald in the Washington, D.C.–based legal journal *Legal Times*, refers to Kennedy in his pre-Court days as a "Sacramento lawyer–lobbyist" who, for no pay, traveled the state on behalf of then–Governor Ronald Reagan's anti-tax initiative. The initiative did not pass, but Kennedy, as Freiwald wrote, "won a soft spot in the heart of the governor. Not long after Kennedy's pro bono [gratuitous] work on the anti-tax initiative, Governor Reagan was in touch with the Nixon White House, urging the pres-

ident to consider Kennedy, then thirty-eight, for a nomina-
tion to the prestigious U.S. Court of Appeals for the 9th
Circuit. Ultimately, it was President Gerald Ford who gave
Kennedy the nod in March of 1975. But several officials
involved in the judicial selection process, as well as
Kennedy's friends, confirm that Kennedy was viewed as
Ronald Reagan's . . . choice for the 9th Circuit."

Kennedy's father was a legendary Sacramento lobbyist
whose clientele Kennedy inherited when his father died
unexpectedly in 1963. Kennedy's clients included Schenley,
California Association of Dispensing Opticians, Capitol
Records, GRT Corporation, and the National Association of
Alcoholic Beverage Importers. Freiwald writes that "it was in
the money-soaked world of politics in the capital of the
nation's most popular and diverse state that Anthony
Kennedy came of age, doing well by his clients, meeting the
right people, and setting in motion the events that would cul-
minate in his Supreme Court appointment."

Freiwald continued, "Kennedy contributed thousands of
dollars on behalf of his clients to state and local elected officials. [He] entertained clients and legislators at exclusive
restaurants and country clubs in Sacramento and San
Francisco, [charging] some of his golfing fees and club mem-
berships to his lobbying clients. Kennedy's lobbying records
also show that he had a penchant for purchasing hundreds of
dollars' worth of 'bottled liquor for entertainment' when woo-
ing legislators and clients. In the 'clubby' circle of
Sacramento lawyers-lobbyists, Kennedy 'was one of the guys
you know,' recalls Clayton Jackson, now one of Sacramento's
highest-paid lobbyists."

The long and short of it was that Anthony Kennedy was
a "go to" guy, someone corporations with money went to in
order to get things done. And boy, he certainly got things
done (as Vice President Dick Cheney would say, "big-time")
for his party, the Republican Party, in *Bush v. Gore*.

The aforementioned political backgrounds of some of the members of the Supreme Court, and the reminder they are all simply lawyers who wear black robes, is set forth only to reduce the Justices down to their true dimensions—nine ordinary human beings who are subject to all the infirmities that afflict mankind. The five Justices who, I believe you will find, literally stole a presidential election from the American people, did so not because they are lawyers or politicians, but because like so many among us, including those of the highest station in life and the bluest of pedigree, they had, incubating inside of them, the most squalid of characters, a lowness that may never have manifested itself if they had never been presented with this situation. If anyone believes that a decent and honorable human being could have done something as horrendous as these Justices did, I say to you that you are very mistaken. Indeed, I told my daughter, Wendy, that what these Justices ended up doing was so monumentally base, so extraordinarily wrong and dishonorable that I wasn't gifted enough as a writer to describe it. (I view myself as a trial lawyer who happens to be a writer, not a writer who happens to be a trial lawyer.) I told her that in view of the immense, measureless consequences of their act, and the greatness of their sin, it would take a Tolstoy, a Shakespeare, a Hemingway, to give people an illuminating glimpse into the interior of the soul and marrow of these five Justices. But I suspect that a great writer would be trying to give verbal flesh to the fact that the five Justices had absolutely no regard, no respect, for fifty million Americans, whose votes for Vice President Gore they knew they were erasing as if never cast; no appreciation for, nor sense of responsibility to, the majestic and towering office they occupied; no concern at all about a betrayal of trust on their part that may be unparalleled in the recorded annals of American history.

One could say to me, "Mr. Bugliosi, if what you say is true, how could it be that five out of nine human beings on the Court could have such a low character? The law of probability defeats your position." This argument is quite similar to one made to me by a young woman a half-year ago about the essential goodness of people, which is the generally accepted view, even by most philosophers, of humankind. "Deep down," one always hears, "most people are good." But I could write a very long treatise on how people are just wonderful; that is, until their self-interest is involved. When the latter happens, watch out. I told the young lady that in no more than fifteen seconds I could demonstrate to her not only that she was wrong but that she herself already, prior to my demonstration, never truly believed what she was telling me. Try me, she challenged.[3] I told her to imagine coming out of her home one day and seeing her car, parked out on the street, having been dented by a passing car. On the windshield is a note from the driver with his name and phone number on it, asking her to call him. Would she be surprised, I asked her. After a short pause, she smiled knowingly to me and said, "Yes." I didn't have to ask her the obvious question—if most people, as she said, are essentially good, why would she be surprised?

My view? Although there are millions upon millions of very wonderful people in the world who do have sufficient character to rise above their own self-interest, they are in the distinct minority. And I say that not because of my intimate exposure to the darkest side of humanity in my years as a criminal prosecutor, but by being an observer, as we all are, of the human condition.

INTRODUCTION

NOTE ONE

"THE COURT HAS been bombarded with thousands of letters from angry Americans, some of whom have sent in their voter registration cards. . . . 'For shame' one letter said. Many messages to the justices have been sarcastic, others more menacing—including one with an illustration of a skull and crossbones . . . Sandra Day O'Connor has told people close to her that in her two decades on the court, she has never seen such anger over a case." (*USA Today*, January 22, 2001, p.1.) I can't imagine why.

NOTE TWO

JUDGES, WITH THE ironic exception of Justices of the United States Supreme Court, must be lawyers. No non-lawyer has ever sat on the U.S. Supreme Court, although Lyndon Johnson did try to get non-lawyer Dean Rusk, his Secretary of State, to accept a nomination to the Court, but Rusk declined.

NOTE THREE

THAT PEOPLE FORM opinions without any thinking
that led up to them—thinking is hard work, they say, that's
why so few people engage in it—and that their opinions can
be exposed as being flawed in a matter of seconds, was also
shown to be apparent in a different context. I am writing
two volumes on the assassination of President John F.
Kennedy. My conclusion is that I believe beyond *all* doubt
that Lee Harvey Oswald killed Kennedy, and beyond all *reasonable* doubt that he acted alone. The latter position, of
course, is one that is at odds with the vast majority of
Americans, who, because of their lack of knowledge about
all the facts of the case, and the massive amount of misinformation they have been fed by conspiracy theorists
(magic bullet, Oswald was a poor shot, etc.), are in no position to form an intelligent opinion about it.

In any event, back in early 1992, a few months after the
factually impoverished and absurd pro-conspiracy movie *JFK*
by Oliver Stone, who seems to have a sweet tooth for silliness, I was speaking to about 600 lawyers at a trial lawyers'
convention on the East Coast. My subject was "Tactics and
Techniques in the Trial of a Criminal Case," not the Kennedy
assassination, but during the question and answer period
that followed, the assassination came up, and I could tell
from the rhetorical nature of the questions that the ques-
tioner believed there was a conspiracy in the assassination. I
proceeded to ask for a show of hands as to how many did not
accept the findings of the Warren Commission. A forest of
hands went up, easily 85–90 percent of the audience. So I
said to them, "What if I could prove to you in one minute or
less that although you are all intelligent people, you're not
thinking intelligently about the Kennedy case?" I could sense
an immediate stirring in the audience. My challenge sound-
ed ridiculous. How could I *prove* in one minute or less that

close to 600 lawyers were not thinking intelligently? A voice from my right front shouted out, "We don't think you can do it." "Okay," I responded, "start looking at your watches." With the clock ticking, I asked for another show of hands as to those who had seen the recent movie, *JFK*, or at any time in the past had ever read any book or magazine article propounding the conspiracy theory or otherwise rejecting the findings of the Warren Commission. Again, a great number of hands went up—about the same, it seemed to me, as the previous hand count. I then told the group that I didn't need a show of hands for my next point. "I'm sure you will all agree," I said, "that before you form an intelligent opinion on a matter in dispute, you should hear both sides of the issue. As the old West Virginia mountaineer said, 'No matter how thin I make my pancakes, they always have two sides.' With that in mind, how many of you have read the Warren Report?" It was embarrassing. Only a few people raised their hands. In less than a minute (one member of the audience later told me it was forty-seven seconds) I had proved my point. The overwhelming majority in the audience had formed an opinion rejecting the findings of the Warren Commission without bothering to read the commission's report. And I hadn't even asked them how many had read the twenty-six volumes of the Warren Commission, just the single volume Warren Report.

There could be no better example of how most people are utterly incapable of rising above their self-interest (even if the self-interest is only perceived and not real, and even if the self-interest is very small), than the response of Republican Party voters, not just to the the Supreme Court decision in *Bush v. Gore*, but to the entire Florida election controversy. Picture 500 people, all Republicans, in a motion picture theater at some point in time before the 2000 election. The movie can be a love story, a drama, a suspense thriller, or what have you, that takes place in Mexico.

In an important part of the movie, there is a presidential election in which party A wins a comfortable majority of the votes—well over a half million, in fact—but because of a centuries-old law that hadn't come into play in over 100 years and that polls always showed the great bulk of Mexicans thought should be repealed, party B, *whom the majority of Mexicans did not want as their president*, wins the election; basically, one could say, on a legal technicality. Not just one or ten or two hundred, but chances are *all 500* people in the theater watching the movie (where we know people traditionally suspend their disbelief and get caught up in the drama unfolding before their eyes) would be very unhappy and have a very unsatisfying feeling about what they just witnessed, since it runs absolutely contrary to what we all believe—that the person with the most votes, the team that scores the most points, et cetera, wins. In fact, the notion of the minority being on top goes in the direction of a totalitarian regime; again, antithetical to everything we believe in. But, of course, the above scenario is the precise situation that happened in the 2000 election, with Gore receiving over 539,000 more votes than Bush in the general election throughout the country.

Now let's look at how these 500 Republican moviegoers reacted in real life. But before we do, let's note that their self-interest could not even have been too great here, since in the previous Democratic administration, one whose policies we can assume Vice-President Gore would continue, as we alluded to earlier there were eight years of prosperity and peace, which were good for Republicans as well as Democrats. And there aren't too many ways, I would think, that you can improve on peace and prosperity. And certainly, no one, but no one, was suggesting that Governor George Bush was the greatest candidate for President this nation ever had and the nation just absolutely *had* to have him as their president. Yet basically, merely because he was a member of the same political party as they, the over-whelming majority of the 500 Republican moviegoers threw all their sense of empathy and fairness, all civility, out the window, and even though they only had a lead of just 300 or so votes in Florida (I assure you, they would have acted the same identical way if their lead were only five votes), instead of walking away quietly with their tail between their legs, knowing they were extremely lucky to win on a tech-nicality, they were not unhappy at all. In fact, most turned into angry and vociferous assailants of Democrats in gener-al, and Gore in particular, for challenging the election results (even though everything Gore did was authorized by law), with many calling him obscenities and a "thief" and in general treating him and his party like villains and sore los-ers. In fact, it was reported that right-wing legislative thug Tom Delay (as repugnant as I find Delay to be, *even* he, in that group of 500 Republican moviegoers, would not have liked what he was seeing on the screen) had some of his people screaming and pounding on the door of the Dade County canvassing board, demanding a stop to the recount. Mankind is essentially good, right?

Now let's go back to the theater. In a section of Sonora, one of the Mexican states, there was a ballot in the federal election that was confusing to many voters, particularly older folks, and because of it, several thousand ended up voting not for the person they intended to, Party A (the one who won the majority of votes in the country), but Party C, someone whose politics and views they absolutely loathed. If they hadn't made that mistake, and if they had voted the way they intended to vote, and thought they were voting, not only would Party A have won in the state of Sonora, but because of it, he would have won the national election. Again, all 500 Republican moviegoers would be highly dis-turbed by the development in the movie. If their thoughts, sitting in the theater, could be verbalized, they'd be saying,

"Hey, this just isn't right. These poor people made a mistake. The wrong guy ended up winning here. There ought to be something that can be done about this."

Again, this is precisely what happened in Palm Beach County with the so-called butterfly ballot. The ballot was, actually, a little confusing (in that vertically, Buchanan's name was closer to Bush's name than was Gore's), not just to the elderly Jewish folks who voted for Pat Buchanan instead of whom they intended to vote for, Gore, but for many younger people who said they voted for Buchanan by mistake. For example, forty-eight year old Ken Weitz, who erroneously voted for Buchanan, told *Newsweek* (November 20, 2000) that the ballot "was anything but crystal clear." Weitz designs and builds million-dollar homes. Andre Fladell, a fifty-two year old Jewish chiropractor, told *Time* magazine (November 20, 2000) that on the way out of the elementary school where he voted, when he heard people complain that the ballot confused them, he assumed they had not paid enough attention. But at lunch later with friends, he broke into a cold sweat when he heard them describe the correct punch hole for Gore-Lieberman, and Fladell realized that he too had inadvertently voted for Pat Buchanan. "A ballot is supposed to lead me to my vote," he said. "This one led me away."

It was estimated that at least 3,000 of the 3,400 votes Buchanan got in heavily Democratic Palm Beach County (far more than he got in any other of Florida's sixty-seven counties) were intended to be votes for Gore, votes that easily would have given the election to Gore. In addition, 19,235 out of the 462,888 voters in Palm Beach County "double punched" their ballots, mostly for Gore and Buchanan, rendering all of them invalid. Buchanan (one of the very few right-wingers for whom—putting aside some of his positions—I have some respect) himself said at the time: "Most of those are probably not my votes, and that may be enough to give the margin to Mr. Gore."*

How did the 500 Republican moviegoers, very sympathetic to the mistake in Sonora, react to the Palm Beach situation, where their self-interest was involved? Not only did they have no sympathy for the Palm Beach voters, but instead heaped scorn and ridicule upon them. "If they're too stupid to read a ballot, they shouldn't be voting in the first place." "They can punch a bingo card properly, but not a ballot. I have no sympathy for them." "If they made a mistake, that's their problem, not ours." These were the type of remarks one constantly heard from Republicans all over the country.

It should be noted parenthetically that this tough stance toward the mistake of the Palm Beach residents is, once again, in total opposition to our culture. I'm not suggesting that the erroneous votes for Buchanan should have been changed to a vote for Gore, but the position that Republicans have taken is wrong on several fronts, although I've yet to hear one Republican mention even one of the following points. One, as a general rule in our daily lives, when one makes an innocent mistake, nearly always the party with whom you're dealing permits you to rectify it. For example, you buy a gift for a friend at Christmas thinking she'd like it or need it, and you find out she doesn't like

---

* So not only did a century-old technicality enable Bush to win the national election even though he lost by over a half million votes, but he won Florida by mistake. Yet there were human mutants who loudly protested outside the Vice-President's home in Washington, D.C., before the election was over, demanding that he "get out of Cheney's home." In their partial defense, it is unlikely that the collective IQ of these people was higher than room temperature. But even these mutants, if they were among the 500 moviegoers, would be thinking to themselves, if their conduct were being depicted on film, "where do these people get the guts to act this way? Can you even *buy* guts like this?"

it or already has it. When you take it back to the store, they refund your money. They don't say, "If you're so stupid that you don't know what your friend likes or needs, that's your problem, not ours." (Even in those situations where the situation cannot be rectified—e.g., a student, by mistake, shows up half an hour late for an exam. The teacher, though not granting the student the extra half an hour, can normally be expected to say he is sorry and he wishes he could give the student more time, but it would establish a bad precedent.)

Secondly, the lenient and sympathetic treatment towards the mistakes of others is so much a part of our culture (unless peoples' self-interest is involved) that in some situations it is even a complete legal defense to a crime. One example, among several: If someone takes the personal property of another under the mistaken belief that he, the taker, owns it, he obviously has to return it but he is not guilty of the crime of theft.

And finally, the Republican argument about the Palm Beach voters (If they made a mistake, that's too bad, they have to pay for it) not only isn't—as we've seen—the way honest, innocent mistakes are treated in life, but even in those situations where one does have to pay for his mistake, only the person making the mistake suffers. But here, the mistake of the Palm Beach voters caused fifty million people who voted for Al Gore to lose their votes.

Not one of the points I've just mentioned requires any thinking at all. But ask yourself if you heard even one of the aforementioned points being made by any of your Republican friends. The answer, I'm relatively sure, is no. All we've heard from the Republicans is scorn and ridicule and callousness for the poor folks in Palm Beach, even the very elderly ones, who mistakenly voted for the wrong candidate.

I simply relate all of the above to illustrate just how "essentially good" people are when their self-interest, even when it is limited, is at stake. Under those circumstances, most people are not very nice at all.

There was enormous, not limited, self-interest behind the votes of the five Justices who delivered the election to Bush. And they were able to do what they did because at their core, and at their moment of truth, their character came up seriously wanting.

NONE DARE
CALL IT TREASON

by

VINCENT BUGLIOSI

IN THE DECEMBER 12 ruling by the U.S. Supreme Court handing the election to George Bush, the Court committed the unpardonable sin of being a knowing surrogate for the Republican Party instead of being an impartial arbiter of the law.[1] If you doubt this, try to imagine Al Gore's and George Bush's roles being reversed and ask yourself if you can conceive of Justice Antonin Scalia and his four conservative brethren issuing an emergency order on December 9 stopping the counting of ballots (at a time when Gore's lead had shrunk to 154 votes) on the grounds that if it continued, Gore could suffer "irreparable harm," and then subsequently, on December 12, bequeathing the election to Gore on equal protection grounds. If you can, then I suppose you can also imagine seeing a man jumping away from his own shadow, Frenchmen no longer drinking wine.

From the beginning, Bush desperately sought, as it were, to prevent the opening of the door, the looking into the box—unmistakable signs that he feared the truth. In a nation that prides itself on openness, instead of the Supreme Court doing everything within its power to find a legal way to open the door and box, they did the precise

---

[1] All numbers refer to Amplifications beginning on p.63.

opposite in grasping, stretching and searching mightily for a way, any way at all, to aid their choice for president, Bush, in the suppression of the truth, finally settling, in their judicial coup d'état, on the untenable argument that there was a violation of the Fourteenth Amendment's equal protection clause—the Court asserting that because of the various standards of determining the voter's intent in the Florida counties, voters were treated unequally, since a vote disqualified in one county (the so-called undervotes, which the voting machines did not pick up) may have been counted in another county, and vice versa. Accordingly, the Court reversed the Florida Supreme Court's order that the undervotes be counted, effectively delivering the presidency to Bush.

Now, in the equal protection cases I've seen, the aggrieved party, the one who is being harmed and discriminated against, almost invariably brings the action. But no Florida voter I'm aware of brought any action under the equal protection clause claiming he was disenfranchised because of the different standards being employed. What happened here is that Bush leaped in and tried to profit from a hypothetical wrong inflicted on someone else. Even assuming Bush had this right,[2] the very core of his petition to the Court was that he himself would be harmed by these different standards. But would he have? If we're to be governed by common sense, the answer is no. The reason is that just as with flipping a coin you end up in rather short order with as many heads as tails, there would be a "wash" here for both sides, i.e., there is no reason to believe that there wouldn't be just as many Bush as Gore votes that would be counted in one county yet disqualified in the next. (Even if we were to assume, for the sake of argument, that the wash wouldn't end up exactly, 100 percent even, we'd still be dealing with the rule of *de minimis non curat lex*—the law does not concern itself with trifling matters.) So what harm to Bush was the Court so passionately trying to prevent by its ruling other than the real one: that he would be harmed by the truth as elicited from a full counting of the undervotes?

And if the Court's five-member majority was concerned not about Bush but the voters themselves, as they fervently claimed to be, then under what conceivable theory would they, in effect, tell these voters, "We're so concerned that *some* of you undervoters may lose your vote under the different Florida county standards that we're going to solve the problem by making sure that *none* of you undervoters have your votes counted"? Isn't this exactly what the Court did?

Gore's lawyer, David Boies, never argued either of the above points to the Court. Also, since Boies already knew (from language in the December 9 emergency order of the Court) that Justice Scalia, the Court's right-wing ideologue; his Pavlovian puppet, Clarence Thomas, who doesn't even try to create the impression that he's thinking; and three other conservatives on the Court (William Rehnquist, Sandra Day O'Connor and Anthony Kennedy) intended to deodorize their foul intent by hanging their hat on the anemic equal protection argument, wouldn't you think that he and his people would have come up with at least three or four strong arguments to expose it for what it was—a legal gimmick that the brazen, shameless majority intended to invoke to perpetrate a judicial hijacking in broad daylight? And made sure that he got into the record of his oral argument all of these points? Yet, remarkably, Boies only managed to make one good equal protection argument, and that one near the very end of his presentation, and then only because Justice Rehnquist (not at Boies's request, I might add) granted him an extra two minutes. If Rehnquist hadn't given him the additional two minutes, Boies would have sat down without getting even one good equal protection argument into the record.

This was Boies's belated argument: "Any differences as to how this standard [to determine voter intent] is interpreted have a lot less significance in terms of what votes are counted or not counted than simply the differences in machines that exist throughout the counties of Florida." A more powerful way to make Boies's argument would have been to point out to the Court the *reductio ad absurdum* of the equal protection argument. If none of the undervotes were counted because of the various standards to count them, then to be completely consistent the Court would have had no choice but to invalidate the entire Florida election, since there is no question that votes lost in some counties because of the method of voting would have been recorded in others utilizing a different method.[3] How would the conservative majority have gotten around that argument without buckling on the counting of the undervotes? Of course, advice after a mistake is like medicine after death. And as we shall see, no matter what Boies argued, the five conservative Justices had already made up their minds. But it would have been delightful to see how these Justices, forced to stare into the noonday sun, would have attempted to avoid a confrontation with the truth.[4]

The Court majority, *after knowingly transforming* the votes of 50 million Americans into nothing and throwing out all of the Florida undervotes (around 60,000), actually wrote that their ruling was intended to preserve "the fundamental right" to vote. This elevates audacity to symphonic and operatic levels. The Court went on to say, after stealing the election from the American people, "None are more conscious of the vital limits on its judicial authority than are the members of this Court, and none stand more in admiration of the Constitution's design to leave the selection of the President to the people." Can you imagine that? As they say, "It's enough to drive you to drink."

What makes the Court's decision even more offensive is that it warmly embraced, of all the bitter ironies, the equal protection clause, a constitutional provision tailor-made for blacks that these five conservative Justices have shown no hospitality to when invoked in lawsuits by black people, the very segment of the population most likely to be hurt by a Bush administration. As University of Southern California law professor Erwin Chemerinsky noted: "The Rehnquist Court almost never uses equal protection jurisprudence except in striking down affirmative action programs [designed to help blacks and minorities]. I can't think of a single instance where Scalia or Thomas has found discrimination against a racial minority, or women, or the aged, or the disabled, to be unconstitutional."

Varying methods to cast and count votes have been going on in every state of the union for the past two centuries, and the Supreme Court has been as silent as a church mouse on the matter, never even hinting that there might be a right under the equal protection clause that was being violated. Georgetown University law professor David Cole said, "[The Court] created a new right out of whole cloth and made sure it ultimately protected only one person— George Bush." The simple fact is that the five conservative Justices did not have a judicial leg to stand on in their blatantly partisan decision. In a feeble, desperate effort to support their decision, the Court cited four of its previous cases as legal precedent. But when one looks up the cases, one finds that not one of them bears even the slightest resemblance to *Bush v. Gore*. In one (*Gray v. Sanders*), the state of Georgia had a system where the vote of each citizen counted for less and less as the population of his or her county increased. In another (*Moore v. Ogilvie*), the residents of smaller counties in Illinois were able to form a new party to elect candidates, something residents of larger counties could not do. Another (*Reynolds v. Sims*) was an apportionment case, and the fourth (*Harper v. Virginia*) involved the payment of a poll tax as a qualification for voting. If a first-year law student ever cited completely inapplicable authority like this, any thoughtful professor would encourage him not to waste two more years trying to become a lawyer. As Yale law professor Akhil Reed Amar noted, the five conservative Justices "failed to cite a single case that, on its facts, comes close to supporting its analysis and result." [5]

If the Court majority had been truly concerned about the equal protection of all voters, the real equal protection violation, of course, took place when they cut off the counting of the undervotes. As indicated, that very act denied the 50 million Americans who voted for Gore the right to have their votes count at all. It misses the point to argue that the five Justices stole the election only if it turns out that Gore overcame Bush's lead in the undervote recount. We're talking about the moral and ethical culpability of these Justices, and when you do that, the bell was rung at the moment they engaged in their conduct. What happened thereafter cannot unring the bell and is therefore irrelevant. To judge these Justices by the final result rather than by their intentions at the time of their conduct would be like exonerating one who shoots to kill if the bullet misses the victim. With that type of extravagant reasoning, if the bullet goes on and accidentally strikes down a third party who is about to kill another, perhaps the gunman should ultimately be viewed as a hero.

Other than the unprecedented[6] and outrageous nature of what the Court did, nothing surprises me more than how it is being viewed by the legal scholars and pundits who have criticized the opinion. As far as I can determine, most *have* correctly assailed the Court for issuing a ruling that was clearly political. As the December 25 *Time* capsulized it, "A sizable number of critics, from law professors to some of the Court's own members, have attacked the ruling as . . . politically motivated." A sampling from a few law professors: Vanderbilt professor Suzanna Sherry said, "There is really very little way to reconcile this opinion other than that they wanted Bush to win." Yale's Amar lamented that "for Supreme Court watchers this case will be like BC and AD. For many of my colleagues, this was like the day President Kennedy was assassinated. Many of us [had] thought that courts do not act in an openly political fashion." Harvard law professor Randall Kennedy called the decision "outrageous."*

The only problem I have with these critics is that they have merely lost respect for and confidence in the Court. "I have less respect for the Court than before," Amar wrote. The *New York Times* said the ruling appeared "openly political" and that it "eroded public confidence in the Court." Indeed, the always accommodating and obsequious (in all matters pertaining to the High Court, in front of which he regularly appears) Harvard law professor Laurence Tribe, who was Gore's chief appellate lawyer, went even further in the weakness of his disenchantment with the Court. "Even if we disagree" with the Court's ruling, he said, Americans should "rally around the decision."

Sometimes the body politic is lulled into thinking along unreasoned lines. The "conventional wisdom" emerging immediately after the Court's ruling seemed to be that the Court, by its political ruling, had only lost a lot of credibility

---

* The ruling was so bad that it was very difficult to find even conservative legal scholars who supported it, and when the few who attempted to do so stepped up to the plate, their observations were simply pathetic. University of California, Berkeley, law professor John Yoo, a former law clerk for Thomas, wrote that "we should balance the short-term hit to the court's legitimacy with whether...it was in the best interest of the country to end the electoral crisis." Translation: If an election is close, it's better for the Supreme Court to pick the President, *whether or not he won the election*, than to have the dispute resolved in the manner prescribed by law. Pepperdine Law School's Douglas Kmiec unbelievably wrote that "the ruling of the US Supreme Court was not along partisan or ideological lines," and that its ruling "protected our cherished democratic tradition with a soundly reasoned, per curiam voice of restraint." I won't dignify this with a translation.

and altitude in the minds of many people. But these critics of the ruling, even those who flat-out say the Court "stole" the election, apparently have not stopped to realize the inappropriateness of their tepid position vis-à-vis what the Court did. You mean you can steal a presidential election and your only retribution is that some people don't have as much respect for you, as much confidence in you? That's all? If, indeed, the Court, as the critics say, made a politically motivated ruling (which it unquestionably did), this is tantamount to saying, and can *only* mean, that the Court did not base its ruling on the law. And if this is so (which again, it unquestionably is), this means that these five Justices *deliberately and knowingly* decided to nullify the votes of the 50 million Americans who voted for Al Gore and to steal the election for Bush. Of course, nothing could possibly be more serious in its enormous ramifications. The stark reality, and I say this with every fiber of my being, is that the institution Americans trust the most to protect its freedoms and principles committed one of the biggest and most serious crimes this nation has ever seen—pure and simple, the theft of the presidency. And by definition, the perpetrators of this crime *have* to be denominated criminals.

Since the notion of five Supreme Court Justices being criminals is so alien to our sensibilities and previously held beliefs, and since, for the most part, people see and hear, as Thoreau said, what they expect to see and hear, most readers will find my characterization of these Justices to be intellectually incongruous. But make no mistake about it, I think my background in the criminal law is sufficient to inform you that Scalia, Thomas et al. are criminals in the very *truest* sense of the word.

Essentially, there are two types of crimes: *malum prohibitum* (wrong because they are prohibited) crimes, more popularly called "civil offenses" or "quasi crimes," such as selling liquor after a specified time of day, hunting during the off-season, gambling, etc.; and *malum in se* (wrong in themselves) crimes. The latter, such as robbery, rape, murder and arson, are the only true crimes. *Without exception, they all involve morally reprehensible conduct.* Even if there were no law prohibiting such conduct, one would know (as opposed to a *malum prohibitum* crime) it is wrong, often evil. Although the victim of most true crimes is an individual (for example, a person robbed or raped), such crimes are considered to be "wrongs against society." This is why the plaintiff in all felony criminal prosecutions is either the state (*People of the State of California v.* _____) or the federal government (*United States of America v.* _____).

No technical true crime was committed here by the five conservative Justices only because no Congress ever dreamed of enacting a statute making it a crime to steal a presidential election. It is so far-out and unbelievable that there was no law, then, for these five Justices to have violated by their theft of the election.[7] But if what these Justices did was not "morally reprehensible" and a "wrong against society," what would be? In terms, then, of natural law and justice—the protoplasm of all eventual laws on the books—these five Justices are criminals in every *true* sense of the word, and in a fair and just world belong behind prison bars as much as any American white-collar criminal who ever lived. Of course, the right-wing extremists who have saluted the Court for its theft of the election are the same type of people who feel it is perfectly all right to have a mandatory minimum sentence of ten years in a federal penitentiary for some poor black in the ghetto who is in possession of just fifty grams of crack cocaine, even if he was not selling it. [21 U.S.C. §841(b)(1)(A)(iii)]

Though the five Justices clearly are criminals, no one is treating them this way. As I say, even those who were outraged by the Court's ruling have only lost respect for them. And for the most part the nation's press seems to have already forgotten and/or forgiven. Within days, the Court's ruling was no longer the subject of Op-Ed pieces. Indeed, just five days after its high crime, the caption of an article by Jean Guccione in the *Los Angeles Times* read, "The Supreme Court Should Weather This Storm." The following day an AP story noted that Justice Sandra Day O'Connor, on vacation in Arizona, had fired a hole-in-one on the golf course.

The lack of any valid legal basis for their decision and, most important, the fact that it is inconceivable they would have ruled the way they did for Gore, proves, *on its face*, that the five conservative Republican Justices were up to no good. Therefore, not one stitch of circumstantial evidence beyond this is really necessary to demonstrate their felonious conduct and state of mind. (The fact that O'Connor, per the *Wall Street Journal*, said before the election that she wanted to retire but did not want to do so if a Democrat would be selecting her successor, that Thomas's wife is working for the conservative Heritage Foundation to help handle the Bush transition and that Scalia's two sons work for law firms representing Bush is all unneeded trivia. We already know, without this, exactly what happened.)[8] But for those who want more, let me point out that there is no surer way to find out what parties meant than to see what they have done. And like typical criminals, the felonious five left their incriminating fingerprints everywhere, showing an unmistakable consciousness of guilt on their part.

1. Under Florida case and statutory law, when the Florida Supreme Court finds that a challenge to the certified result of an election is justified, it has the power to "provide *any* relief appropriate under the circumstances" (§102.168(8) of the Florida Election Code). On Friday, December 8, the Florida court, so finding, ordered a manual recount (authorized under §102.166(4)(c) of the

Florida Election Code) of all disputed ballots (around 60,000) throughout the entire state. As a *New York Times* editorial reported, "The manual recount [9] was progressing smoothly and swiftly Saturday. . .with new votes being recorded for both Vice President Al Gore and Governor George W. Bush. . .serving the core democratic principle that every legal vote should be counted" when, in midafternoon, the US Supreme Court "did a disservice to the nation's tradition of fair elections by calling a halt" to the recount. The stay (requested by Bush), the *Times* said, appeared "highly political."[10]

Under Supreme Court rules, a stay is supposed to be granted to an applicant (here, Bush) only if he makes a substantial showing that in the absence of a stay, there is a likelihood of "irreparable harm" to him. With the haste of a criminal, Justice Scalia, in trying to justify the Court's shutting down of the vote counting, wrote, unbelievably, that counting these votes would "threaten irreparable harm to petitioner [Bush]. . .by casting a cloud upon what *he* claims to be the legitimacy of *his* election." [Emphasis added.][11] In other words, although the election had not yet been decided, the absolutely incredible Scalia was presupposing that Bush had won the election—indeed, had a *right* to win it— and any recount that showed Gore got more votes in Florida than Bush could "cloud" Bush's presidency. Only a criminal on the run, rushed for time and acting in desperation, could possibly write the embarrassing words Scalia did, language showing that he knew he had no legal basis for what he was doing, but that getting something down in writing, even as intellectually flabby and fatuous as it was, was better than nothing at all. (Rehnquist, Thomas, O'Connor and Kennedy, naturally, joined Scalia in the stay order.)

The *New York Times* observed that the Court gave the appearance by the stay of "racing to beat the clock before an unwelcome truth would come out." Terrance Sandalow, former dean of the University of Michigan Law School and a judicial conservative who opposed *Roe v. Wade* and supported the nomination to the Court of right-wing icon Robert Bork, said that "the balance of harms so unmistakably were on the side of Gore" that the granting of the stay was "incomprehensible," going on to call the stay "an unmistakably partisan decision without any foundation in law." [12]

As Justice John Paul Stevens wrote in opposing the stay, Bush "failed to carry the heavy burden" of showing a likelihood of irreparable harm if the recount continued. In other words, the Court never even had the legal right to grant the stay. "Counting every legally cast vote cannot constitute irreparable harm," Stevens said. "On the other hand, there is a danger that a stay may cause irreparable harm to the respondent [Gore] and, more importantly, the public at large because of the risk that the entry of the stay would be tantamount to a decision on the merits in favor of the applicant. Preventing the recount from being completed will inevitably cast a cloud on the legitimacy of the election." Stevens added what even the felonious five knew but decided to ignore: that it is a "basic principle inherent in our Constitution that every legal vote should be counted." From the wrongful granting of the stay alone, the handwriting was on the wall. Gore was about as safe as a cow in a Chicago stockyard.

In yet another piece of incriminating circumstantial evidence, Scalia, in granting Bush's application for the stay, wrote that "the issuance of the stay suggests that a majority of the Court, while not deciding the issues presented, believe that the petitioner [Bush] has a substantial probability of success." But Antonin, why would you believe this when neither side had submitted written briefs yet (they were due the following day, Sunday, by 4 P.M.), nor had there even been oral arguments (set for 11 A.M. on Monday)? It wouldn't be because you had already made up your mind on what you were determined to do, come hell or high water, would it? Antonin, take it from an experienced prosecutor—you're as guilty as sin. In my prosecutorial days, I've had some worthy opponents. You wouldn't be one of them. Your guilt is so obvious that if I thought more of you I'd feel constrained to blush *for* you.

2. When prosecutors present their circumstantial case against a defendant, they put one speck of evidence upon another until ultimately there is a strong mosaic of guilt. One such small speck is that in its 5-to-4 decision handing the election to Bush, the Court's ruling was set forth in a thirteen-page *"per curiam"* (Latin for "by the court") opinion (followed by concurring and dissenting opinions). Students of the Supreme Court know that *per curiam* opinions are almost always issued for unanimous (9-to-0) opinions in relatively unimportant and uncontroversial cases, or where Justices wish to be very brief. But as *USA Today* pointed out, "Neither was the case here." Again, on the run and in a guilty state of mind, none of the five Justices, even the brazenly shameless Scalia, wanted to sign their name to a majority opinion of the Court reversing the Florida Supreme Court's order to recount the undervotes. A *per curiam* opinion, which is always unsigned, was the answer. It is not even known who wrote the *per curiam* opinion, though it is believed to be O'Connor and/or Kennedy, neither of whose names is mentioned anywhere in the Court's sixty-two-page document.* After they did their dirty work

* It is remarkable that arguably the most consequential and far-reaching decision the U.S. Supreme Court has handed down since its inception on February 1, 1790, one that will undoubtedly alter, for good or for bad, the course of American history, and therefore, world history, was unsigned and anonymously written.

by casting their two votes on the case for their favorite—
two votes that overruled and rendered worthless the votes
of 50 million Americans in fifty states—O'Connor and
Kennedy wanted to stay away from their decision the way
the devil stays away from holy water. Indeed, by their *per
curiam* opinion, it was almost as if the felonious five felt
that since their names would not be on the legally sacrile-
gious opinion, maybe, just maybe, the guilt they knew they
bore would be mitigated, at least somewhat, in posterity.

3. The proof that the Court itself knew its equal protection argument had no merit whatsoever is that when Bush
first asked the Court, on November 22, to consider three
objections of his to the earlier, more limited Florida recount
then taking place, the Court, on November 24, only denied
review on his third objection—yeah, you guessed it, that
the lack of a uniform standard to determine the voter's
intent violated the equal protection clause of the
Fourteenth Amendment. Since the Court, on November
24, felt that this objection was so devoid of merit that it was
unworthy of even being considered by it, what did these
learned Justices subsequently learn about the equal protection clause they apparently did not know in November that
caused them just three weeks later, on December 12, to
embrace and endorse it so enthusiastically? The election
was finally on the line on December 12 and they knew they
had to come up with something, anything, to save the day
for their man.[13]

The bottom line is that nothing is more important in a
democracy than the right to vote. Without it there cannot be
a democracy. And implicit in the right to vote, obviously, is
that the vote be counted. Yet with the election hanging in
the balance, the highest court in the land ordered that the
valid votes of thousands of Americans *not* be counted. That
decision gave the election to Bush.[14] When Justice Thomas

was asked by a skeptical high school student the day after the Court's ruling whether the Court's decision had anything to do with politics, he answered, "Zero." And when a reporter thereafter asked Rehnquist whether he agreed with Thomas, he said, "Absolutely, absolutely." Well, at least we know they can lie as well as they can steal.

4. The Court anchored its knowingly fraudulent decision on the equal protection clause of the Fourteenth Amendment. But wait. Since the electors in the fifty states weren't scheduled to meet and vote until December 18, and the Court's ruling was on December 12, if the Court was really serious about its decision that the various standards in the counties to determine the voter's intent violated the equal protection clause, why not, as Justices Stevens, Souter, Ginsburg and Breyer each noted in separate dissents,[15] simply remand the case back to the Florida Supreme Court with instructions to establish a uniform, statewide standard and continue the recount until December 18? The shameless and shameful felonious five had an answer, which, in a sense, went to the heart of their decision even more than the bogus equal protection argument. The *per curiam* opinion noted that under Title 3 of the United States Code, Section 5 (3 USC § 5), any controversy or contest to determine the selection of electors should be resolved "six days prior to the meeting of the Electoral College," that is, December 12, and inasmuch as the Court issued its ruling at 10 P.M. on December 12, with just two hours remaining in the day, the Court said, "That date [December 12] is upon us," and hence there obviously was no time left to set uniform standards and continue the recount. But there are a multiplicity of problems with the Court's oh-so-convenient escape hatch. Writing in the *Wall Street Journal*, University of Utah law professor Michael McConnell, a legal conservative, pointed out that the

December 12 "deadline" is only a deadline "for receiving 'safe harbor' protection for the state's electors" (i.e., if a state certifies its electors by that date, Congress can't question them), not a federal deadline that must be met. New York University law professor Larry Kramer observed that if a state does not make that deadline, "nothing happens. The counting could continue."

Justice Stevens observed in his dissent that 3 USC §5 "merely provides rules . . . for Congress to follow when selecting among conflicting slates of electors. They do not prohibit a state from counting . . . legal votes until a bonafide winner is determined. Indeed, in 1960, Hawaii appointed two slates of electors and Congress chose to count the one appointed on January 4, 1961, well after the Title 3 deadlines" of December 12 and 18. Thus, Stevens went on to say, even if an equal protection violation is assumed for the sake of argument, "nothing prevents the majority . . . from ordering relief appropriate to remedy that violation without depriving Florida voters of their right to have their votes counted."

But even if December 12 were some kind of actual deadline, nothing was sillier during this whole election debate than the talking heads on television, many of whom were lawyers who should have known better, treating the date as if it were sacrosanct and set in stone (exactly what the Supreme Court majority, trying to defend their indefensible position, said). In the real world, mandatory dates always have an elliptical clause attached to them, "unless there is good cause for extending the date." I cannot be accused of hyperbole when I say that perhaps no less than thousands of times a day in courthouses throughout the country, mandatory ("shall") dates to do this or that (file a brief, a motion, commence a trial, etc.) are waived by the court on the representation of one party alone that he needs more time. If extending the December 12 (or the December 18 date, for that matter)[16] deadline for a few days for the counting of votes to determine who the rightful winner of a presidential election is does not constitute a sufficient cause for a short extension of time, then what in the world does?[17] No one has said it better than columnist Thomas Friedman: "The five conservative Justices essentially ruled that the sanctity of dates, even meaningless ones, mattered more than the sanctity of votes, even meaningful ones. The Rehnquist Court now has its legacy: In calendars we trust." In other words, to Scalia and his friends, speed was more important than justice. More important than accuracy. Being the strong-armed enforcer of deadlines, even inconsequential ones, was more important to these five Justices than being the nation's protector and guardian of the right to vote.

What could be more infuriating than Chief Justice Rehnquist, who knew he was setting up a straw man as counterfeit as the decision he supported, writing that the recount "could not possibly be completed" in the two hours remaining on December 12? The Supreme Court improperly stops the recounting of the votes from Saturday afternoon to Tuesday, December 12, at 10 P.M., then has the barefaced audacity to say that Gore ran out of time? This type of maddening sophistry is enough, as the expression goes, to piss off a saint. How dare these five pompous asses do what they did?

It should be noted that the recount that commenced on Saturday morning, December 9, was scheduled to conclude by 2 P.M. that Sunday, and the vote counters were making excellent progress. For example, as reported in the December 10 New York Times, for the 9,000 Miami-Dade County ballots being counted, eight county court judges counting 1,000 ballots an hour, had, by midday Saturday, "gone through more than a third of the ballots [when Scalia stepped in], and expected to finish by nightfall." So the Court's extending the deadline to December 18 would have provided ample time for the Florida Supreme Court to promulgate a uniform standard, finish the vote-counting in a day or so, and even allow for judicial review. As Justice Ruth Bader Ginsburg observed concerning this last point, "Notably, the Florida Supreme Court has produced two substantial decisions within twenty-nine hours of oral argument." Justice Breyer wrote that the alleged equal protection "deficiency. . .could easily be remedied." But that's assuming the felonious five wanted a remedy. They did not. All of the above are further indicia of their guilty state of mind.

5. If there are two sacred canons of the right-wing in America and ultraconservative Justices like Scalia, Thomas and Rehnquist, it's their ardent federalism, i.e., promotion of states' rights (Rehnquist, in fact, wrote in his concurring opinion about wanting, wherever possible, to "defer to the decisions of state courts on issues of state law"), and their antipathy for Warren Court activist judges. So if it weren't for their decision to find a way, any way imaginable, to appoint Bush president, their automatic predilection would have been to stay the hell out of Florida's business. The fact that they completely departed from what they would almost reflexively do in ninety-nine out of a hundred other cases is again persuasive circumstantial evidence of their criminal state of mind.

6. Perhaps nothing Scalia et al. did revealed their consciousness of guilt more than the total lack of legal stature they reposed in their decision. Appellate court decisions, particularly those of the highest court in the land, *all* enunciate and stand for legal principles. Not just litigants but the courts themselves cite prior holdings as support for a legal proposition they are espousing. But the Court knew that its ruling (that differing standards for counting votes

violate the equal protection clause) could not possibly be a constitutional principle cited in the future by themselves, other courts or litigants. Since different standards for counting votes exist throughout the fifty states (e.g., Texas counts dimpled chads, California does not), forty-four out of the fifty states do not have uniform voting methods, and voting equipment and mechanisms in all states necessarily vary in design, upkeep and performance, to apply the equal protection ruling of *Bush v. Gore* would necessarily invalidate virtually all elections throughout the country.

This, obviously, was an extremely serious problem for the felonious five to deal with. What to do? Not to worry. Are you ready for this one? By that I mean, are you sitting down, since if you're standing, this is the type of thing that could affect your physical equilibrium. Unbelievably, the Court wrote that its ruling was "*limited to the present circumstances*, for the problem of equal protection in election processes generally presents many complexities." (That's pure, unadulterated moonshine. The ruling sets forth a very simple, noncomplex proposition—that if there are varying standards to count votes, this violates the equal protection clause of the Fourteenth Amendment.) In other words, the Court, in effect, was saying its ruling "only applied to those future cases captioned *Bush v. Gore*. In all other equal protection voting cases, litigants should refer to prior decisions of this court." Of the thousands of potential equal protection voting cases, the Court was only interested in, and eager to grant relief to, one person and one person only, George W. Bush.[18] Is there any limit to the effrontery and shamelessness of these five right-wing Justices? Answer: No. This point number six here, all alone and by itself, clearly and unequivocally shows that the Court knew its decision was not based on the merits or the law, and was solely a decision to appoint George Bush president.

THE RIGHT WING, the very people who wanted to impeach Earl Warren, have now predictably taken to arguing that one shouldn't attack the Supreme Court as I am because it can only harm the image of the Court, which we have to respect as the national repository for, and protector of, the rule of law, the latter being a sine qua non to a structured, nonanarchistic society. This is just so much drivel. Under what convoluted theory do we honor the rule of law by ignoring the violation of it (here, the sacred, inalienable right to vote of all Americans) by the Supreme Court? With this unquestioning subservience-to-authority theory, I suppose the laws of the Third Reich—such as requiring Jews to wear a yellow Star of David on their clothing—should have been respected and followed by the Jews. Blacks should have respected Jim Crow laws in the first half of the twentieth century. Naturally, these conservative exponents of not harming the Supreme Court, even though the Court stole a federal election disenfranchising 50 million American citizens, are the same people who felt no similar hesitancy savaging the president of the United States not just day after day, but week after week, month after month, yes, even year after year for having a private and consensual sexual affair and then lying about it. And this was so even though the vitriolic and never-ending attacks crippled the executive branch of government for months on end, causing incalculable damage to the office of the presidency and to this nation, both internally and in the eyes of the world. Indeed, many of them are delighted to hound and go after the president even after he leaves office.

These five Justices, by their conduct, have forfeited the right to be respected, and only by treating them the way they deserve to be treated can we demonstrate our respect for the rule of law they defiled, and insure that their successors will not engage in similarly criminal conduct.

Why, one may ask, have I written this article? I'll tell you why. I'd like to think, like most people, that I have a sense of justice. In my mind's eye, these five Justices have gotten away with murder, and I want to do whatever I can to make sure that they pay dearly for their crime. Though they can't be prosecuted, I want them to know that there's at least one American out there (and hopefully many more because of this article) who knows (not thinks, but knows) precisely who they are. I want these five Justices to know that because of this article, which I intend to send to each one of them by registered mail, there's the exponential possibility that when many Americans look at them in the future, they'll be saying, "Why are these people in robes seated above me? They all belong behind bars." I want these five Justices to know that this is America, not a banana republic, and in the United States of America, you simply cannot get away with things like this.

At a minimum, I believe that the Court's inexcusable ruling will severely stain its reputation for years to come, perhaps decades. This is very unfortunate. As Justice Stevens wrote in his dissent: "Although we may never know with complete certainty the identity of the winner of this year's presidential election, the identity of the loser is perfectly clear. It is the nation's confidence in [this Court] as an impartial guardian of the rule of law." Considering the criminal intention behind the decision, legal scholars and historians should place this ruling above the Dred Scott case (*Scott v. Sandford*) and *Plessy v. Ferguson* in egregious sins of the Court. The right of every American citizen to have his or her vote counted, and for Americans (not five unelected Justices) to choose their President was callously and I say criminally jettisoned by the Court's majority to further its own political ideology. If there is such a thing as a judicial hell, these five Justices won't have to worry about heating bills in their future. Scalia and Thomas in particular are not only a disgrace to the judiciary but to the legal profession, for years being nothing more than transparent shills for the right wing of the Republican Party. If the softest pillow is a clear conscience, these five Justices are in for some hard nights. But if they aren't troubled by what they did, then we're dealing with judicial sociopaths, people even more frightening than they already appear to be.

The Republican Party had a good candidate for president, John McCain. Instead, it nominated perhaps the most unqualified person ever to become president,[19] and with the muscular, thuggish help of the Court, forced Bush down the throats of more than half the nation's voters. As Linda Greenhouse wrote in the *New York Times*, when Rehnquist administers the presidential oath of office to Bush on January 20, for the first time in our nation's history the Chief Justice will not just be a prop in the majestic ceremony but a player. Rehnquist will be swearing in someone he made sure would be president. Obscenity has its place in a free and open society, but it's in the seedy, neon-light part of town, not on the steps of the nation's Capitol being viewed by millions of Americans on television screens throughout the land.

That an election for an American president can be stolen by the highest court in the land under the deliberate pretext of an inapplicable constitutional provision has got to be one of the most frightening and dangerous events ever to have occurred in this country. Until this act—which is treasonous, though again not technically,[20] in its sweeping implications—is somehow rectified (and I do not know how this can be done), can we be serene about continuing to place the adjective "great" before the name of this country?

NONE DARE
CALL IT TREASON

AMPLIFICATION ONE

THERE CAN BE no reasonable question that U.S. Supreme Court Justices Rehnquist, Scalia, Thomas, O'Connor, and Kennedy did not act impartially in the case of *Bush v. Gore*, and therefore violated the oath of office they took upon ascending to the highest court in the land. The following is the oath they took, as set forth in Section 453 of Title 28 of the United States Code: "I, _____ _____, do solemnly swear (or affirm) that I will administer justice without respect to persons, and do equal right to the poor and to the rich, and that *I will faithfully and impartially discharge and perform all the duties incumbent upon me* as a justice of the United States Supreme Court under the Constitution and laws of the United States. So help me God." (Emphasis added.)

What good is an oath of office by Supreme Court justices if the violation of said oath carries no punishment for the offender? Remarkably, no sanctions nor punishment for a violation of 28 U.S.C.§453 is set forth in the United States Code.

On the night of the Supreme Court decision, Lis Wiehl, a political moderate who is a constitutional law professor at the University of Washington in Seattle, was on *Hardball*, the cable television show hosted by fast-talking Chris Matthews. When Ms. Wiehl pointed out that the 5-4 decision "split down party lines," which, she said, "makes it look political," Matthews quickly retorted "And the Florida Supreme Court [6 of whose 7 members are Democrats], when it ruled straight Democratic [actually, although its November 21 ruling was unanimous, its December 8 ruling was 4-3 with a strong dissent by Chief Justice Charles T. Wells] was political or not as you see it?" Ms. Wiehl answered, "I don't think it was political. I think they were interpreting the law," whereupon Matthews instantly gave Ms. Wiehl a very disbelieving smirk that clearly said, "Oh please, c'mon. You can't be serious."

With 95 percent of the American television public getting their intellectual sustenance from game shows and sit-coms, should the remaining 5 percent have to be subjected to vapid foolishness like this? This isn't *Hardball*, this is *Sillyball*. Based on this exchange between Matthews and his guest, apparently Matthews believes that you determine if a decision is political or not by seeing if it favors the person who belongs to the same political party that the justices do. But this is incredibly immature and simplistic thinking. Should you have to be told, Chris, that what you have to do is look at what the justices *did*, not what their political affiliation is. And if what they *did* is so outrageous and lacking in legal support, and it would be impossible to imagine their ruling the same way for the other party, then and only then does one start to deduce that politics must have been behind the ruling. The Florida Supreme Court did nothing at all from which any rational inference of a political motivation could be inferred. That is, unless one wants to rely on the impressive logic of Mr. Matthews.

THERE SEEMS TO be something intrinsically question-able in the application of the equal protection clause to this case. If we're to believe the opinion of the U.S. Supreme Court Justices, their *only* concern was with the voters whose rights, they claimed, were negated by a violation of the equal protection clause resulting from the differing standards to count votes in the various counties of Florida. Nowhere do they utter one word of concern for George Bush's rights or say that his rights were violated. Yet they resolved the matter by denying *all* the undervoters in the state of Florida (the ones they expressed so much concern for) the right to have their votes counted, and gave Bush, whose rights they never once said they were trying to pro-tect, all the benefits from the alleged discrimination against the undervoters. Is there something wrong and crazy going on here, or am I just getting old?

Apart from the seeming incongruity of the above, there's a fundamental legal problem that, remarkably, the Gore side never broached with the Court, and the Court, on its own, never seemed to consider. It deals with the legal con-cept known as "standing to sue." It can become a rather complex area of the law, but its essence was stated in the U.S. Supreme Court case of *Werth v. Seldin*, 422 U.S. 490, 498 (1974): "The question of standing is whether the liti-gant is *entitled* to have the court decide the merits of the dispute."

If, for instance, A rear-ends B's car with the front end of his car, obviously only A (not C, some third party stranger) would have standing (be entitled) to sue B.

Did Bush have standing here? I asked that question of Erwin Chemerinsky, a widely respected constitutional law professor and Harvard law school graduate who has written over 100 law review articles and three books, *Interpreting the*

Constitution, *Federal Jurisdiction*, and *Constitutional Law: Principles and Policies*. In a short, non-legalese response for the readers of this book, here is what he faxed me on February 28, 2001:

"Among the Supreme Court's errors [in *Bush v. Gore*] was not raising the issue of whether George W. Bush had standing to raise the equal protection claim. The law is clear that a person has standing only to raise injuries that he or she personally suffers. Bush's claim was that Florida voters were treated unequally by the counting of votes without standards because identical ballots might be treated differently elsewhere in the state. But since he did not vote in Florida, he would not suffer this injury. Although Gore did not raise this issue, the Supreme Court long has said that standing is a jurisdictional question that courts can and must raise on their own."

In a subsequent telephone conversation with Chemerinsky the same day, I asked him about so-called "third-party standing." He said there are essentially only two types of third party beneficiary exceptions to the standing rule. "One is where," he said, "there is a close relationship between the plaintiff [here, Bush] and the third party [here, the Florida voter], like doctor-patient. All of these types of third-party cases have involved personal relationships, which we do not have here. The other exception is where the third-party is unable to protect his interests in court. Here, however, Florida voters could have gone to court to assert their own rights under the equal protection clause. None did that here. I don't believe George Bush even had standing to bring his lawsuit."

Whether he did or not certainly was an eminently important issue that should have been raised by the lawyers for Gore or the Court on its own. But it was not.

AMPLIFICATION THREE

A TOTAL OF 3,718,305 votes were cast in the Florida election under the Votomatic punch-card system, and 2,353,811 votes were cast under the optical-scan system. The percentage of votes not picked up using the punch-card system was 3.92 percent, the rate under the more modern optical-scan system being only 1.43 percent. Put in other terms, for every 10,000 votes cast, the punch-card system resulted in 250 more nonvotes than the optical-scan system. *Siegel v. LePore*, No. 00-15981. See also Ford Fessenden, "No-Vote Rates Higher in Punch-Card Counts," *New York Times*, December 1.

AMPLIFICATION FOUR

ON THE ISSUE upon which the United States Supreme Court handed the election to Bush, a violation of the equal protection clause of the Fourteenth Amendment, Gore's lawyers simply could not have been any worse. In David Boies's oral argument, I pointed out that absent the extra two minutes he received, he was apparently willing to sit down without making one *good* equal protection argument. And in the fifty-one-page brief by Gore's lawyers on December 10, their final brief to the Supreme Court, instead of coming up with five, six, seven equal protection arguments, separately laid out and powerfully articulated, they came up with just one page (I repeat, one page) of pablum and mishmash that couldn't convince one's own mother.

Not only didn't they make one persuasive equal protection argument but, remarkably, they never cited one single case to support whatever they did say, a cardinal sin among appellate lawyers. For instance, they said that Bush's claim that the lack of uniform standards in the various Florida counties violates the Fourteenth Amendment "simply finds no support in the law," but then they cited no case to support what they had just said, which made their assertion meaningless.

Mainly, the Gore brief lamely argued that the problem was an inherent one and nothing could be done about it ("so long as the count is conducted by humans, it undeniably would be possible to allege some degree of inconsistency in the treatment of individual ballots"), certainly an argument calculated to persuade someone to come over to your side, right? Then they completely missed the point by analogizing these inconsistencies to those that exist when humans interpret any legal standard (e.g., reasonable doubt, negligence, etc.). But although interpretations inevitably vary, legal standards like reasonable doubt and negligence *are* uniform, and therefore *legal standards* could not, obviously, be cited to rebut the Bush argument that different standards to count votes existed in the various Florida counties. The Gore argument was inapplicable.

Then the Gore brief argued that since many other states have different methods of counting votes, Bush's equal protection argument, if embraced, would mean that "these practices [in other states] violate the Fourteenth Amendment." But saying that *other* states may be violating the Fourteenth Amendment, an amorphous argument that goes absolutely nowhere, is not the same as maintaining that if the Court ruled that none of the undervotes were counted in Florida because of the various standards to count them, then to be completely consistent the Court would have no choice but to invalidate the entire Florida election, since it is indisputable that votes lost in some counties because of the method of voting would have been recorded in others utilizing a different method. At least from an argumentation standpoint, this would leave the Court, if it were beholden to logic, with the choice of either invalidating the Florida election and voting all over again, or rejecting Bush's argument that the various standards violated the Fourteenth Amendment.

Why couldn't the Gore lawyers, in their December 10 brief, have shown some spunk and originality by respectfully asking the Court to ask Mr. Bush's lawyers the following morning in oral argument, "What evidence do you have, empirical or otherwise, that the lack of a uniform voting standard in the Florida counties is more likely to hurt Mr. Bush than Mr. Gore?" If such a question were asked, what could Bush's lawyers possibly have said? And if they had no answer, doesn't the equal protection argument go out the window, at least insofar as Bush is concerned? And if the Court wasn't interested in Bush, only in the voters losing their vote because of the different standards, why wasn't the point made in the brief and in oral argument that if, indeed, the Court was concerned about some of these undervoters losing their vote, how would the Court be helping them by ruling that *none* of their votes be counted? Which is exactly what happened when the court stopped the vote counting.

Then Gore's brief said, "If petitioners mean to say that all votes must be tabulated under a fixed and mechanical standard (e.g., the "two-corner-chad rule"), their approach would render unconstitutional the laws of states that hinge the meaning of the ballot on the intent of the voter," and would end up disenfranchising many voters "whose intent was clearly [otherwise] discernible." Now what in the hell does that mean? Was Gore arguing *against* a uniform standard? I thought *everyone* agreed a uniform standard was preferable and the goal.

The one-page Gore rebuttal to the Bush equal protection argument was worse than bad. It was appalling. I have no doubt in my mind that thousands of civil lawyers in the country could have done a far superior job. (It must be reiterated, however, that whatever Gore's lawyers argued, it would have been unavailing with these five Justices, who clearly were determined to make George Bush our next president.) To think that this is what Al Gore (and the fifty million people who voted for him) got for their money is very disturbing.

The Gore team was so bad on the equal protection issue that they didn't even pin the Supreme Court against the wall by pointing out that the Court, in its rulings at least since 1945 (*Akins v. Texas*, 325 U.S. 398), and continuing up to *Bush v. Gore*, had consistently held that the equal protection clause can only be successfully invoked if the discrimination was intentional. For instance, in perhaps the leading case setting forth this doctrine, *Washington v. Davis*, 426 U.S. 229 (1976), the Court, in upholding the constitutionality of a Washington, D.C., police department recruitment test that discriminated against black applicants, discussed a long line of cases following this requirement. Citing, for example, the school desegregation cases, the Court said that "[t]he invidious quality of a law claimed to be racially discriminating must ultimately be traced to a racially discriminating *purpose*. That there are both predominantly black and predominantly white schools in a community is not alone violative of the equal protection clause. The essential element of *de jure* segregation is a current condition of segregation resulting from *intentional* state action."

As recently as *Hunter v. Underwood*, 471 U.S. 222 (1984) and *United States v. Armstrong*, 517 U.S. 456 (1996), in both of which cases Rehnquist, as a Justice in *Hunter* and the chief justice in *Armstrong*, delivered the opinion of the Court, the Court affirmed the rule that mere discrimination against a person or group was insufficient. To trigger equal protection clause protections there has to be a showing that the discrimination was intentional. In *Armstrong*, a selective prosecution case just four years before *Bush v. Gore*, Rehnquist wrote that it was not enough for the respondent (defendant) to demonstrate that the prosecutorial policy had a discriminating effect. He also had to show that the policy "was motivated by a discriminating purpose."

For those who might think that perhaps the requirement of intentional discrimination doesn't apply to voting cases, they would be wrong. In *City of Mobile, Alabama v. Bolden*, 446 U.S. 55 (1980), a class action suit was brought by black citizens of Mobile who alleged that the practice of electing City Commissioners at large (as opposed to from individual districts) unfairly diluted the voting strength of blacks in violation of the equal protection clause. In denying relief to the plaintiffs, the Supreme Court ruled that "only if there is *purposeful* discrimination can there be a violation of the equal protection clause of the Fourteenth Amendment," and the Court found no such intentional discrimination present.

Even assuming all voters in Florida were not treated equally because of the various standards, this unequal treatment only resulted from the individual authorities in each of Florida's sixty-seven counties setting up different standards from each other. Within each county all voters were treated equally. No one in any county could possibly have been thinking about discriminating against residents of other counties. Therefore, the alleged discrimination, if any, was totally unintentional and innocent. So we know that if the Court in *Bush v. Gore* followed its own line of cases, it would have rejected Bush's equal protection argument. As University of Virginia law professor Dick Howard said, the Court's decision was "a remarkable use of the equal protection clause. It is not consistent with anything they have done in the past 25 years. No one even claimed there was intentional discrimination here."

Yet just as remarkably, Gore's lawyers never even raised the issue in their written briefs or oral argument.

The fact that the Supreme Court deliberately departed from the position it had taken on equal protection cases throughout the years is just further evidence that its ruling only had one purpose—to appoint George W. Bush president.

The two main legal names that appeared on the aforementioned December 10, 2000, Gore brief to the United States Supreme Court were David Boies and Laurence Tribe. Tribe is reputed to be the leading constitutional law professor in the country, but by my lights he did an excellent job of concealing this fact during his performance in *Bush v. Gore*. Tribe is the person who made the unbelievable remark that though he didn't agree with the Supreme Court's ruling, Americans should now "rally around the decision." I just think that's deplorable.

As far as Boies is concerned, if I'm going to be candid I have to say that although he seems to be a very nice, pleasant man and quite intelligent, with a photographic memory, and although he may be a superb corporate or business lawyer, he bears no resemblance to what my conception of an effective trial lawyer is.* At least based on what I saw of him in the case of *Bush v. Gore*, not only wasn't Boies a fighter (indeed, he was almost meek), but he wasn't forceful or eloquent at all in making his points. And although he seemed to have a very good grasp of the facts, he seemed completely incapable of drawing powerful, irresistible inferences from those facts that painted his opposition into a corner.

About his not being a fighter at all, when I brought up this observation to a non-lawyer friend, he asked me for an example. During oral argument before the Court on December 11, 2000, when the Justices were taking up Boies's valuable time by constantly interrupting him with a great number of questions, not letting him give his prepared remarks, Boies did nothing at all. I can tell you exactly how someone like Gerry Spence, the preeminent defense attorney in the country, or Roy Black, the top trial lawyer in Florida, or even an appellate lawyer like Alan Dershowitz (Alan, though not a trial lawyer, is a fighter and is articulate) would have handled the situation: "Justice _____, in all deference to this Court, I represent a client whom fifty million Americans voted for, and I *must* make the point that _____." With millions upon millions of people listening by audio hookup, and since this *was* supposed to be the time for oral *argument*, what do you think the Justices would have said? "I'm sorry, Mr. Spence, but we're not going to let you make the point you want to make. Just answer our questions." Hardly.

* For those who feel my saying Boies is quite intelligent yet seemed to be an ineffective advocate is contradictory, let me say that intelligence is hardly the key ingredient of being a top-flight trial lawyer. As a trial lawyer, intelligence is important only in the sense that it allows you to play the game. Without it, you don't even have a ticket into the competitive arena. But beyond that, it doesn't get you very far at all. If it did, out of the close to one million lawyers in the country, we'd have a tremendous number of great trial lawyers, but the reality is that great trial lawyers are about as rare as fishermen who don't exaggerate.

AMPLIFICATION FIVE

IT SHOULD BE noted that the absence of legal precedent for a decision by the Supreme Court is not, per se, a problem. Throughout the years, the Court has been confronted with cases of "first impression." What *is* inexcusable here is that the Court deliberately tried to mislead the readers of its opinion into believing that the four cases it cited legally supported and justified its ruling, which the cases did not do.

AMPLIFICATION SIX

A COMMON REFRAIN among the right wing with respect to the Supreme Court decision in *Bush v. Gore* is that the ruling was not political, but even if it was, what's the big deal? Supreme Court majorities throughout the years have rendered decisions clearly intended to further their own ideology. But such an argument is either ill-informed or deliberate obfuscation. Let's not confuse ideology with politics. Unquestionably, there have been many Supreme Court decisions before *Bush v. Gore* that were ideologically driven; that is, liberal as opposed to conservative. For example, liberals on the court wanting to help, by their ruling, the poor and the disadvantaged; conservatives, those in authority and the well-to-do. Liberals wanting to expand the rights of the criminally accused; conservatives, the rights of the victims. But that's not what we're talking about here. We're talking about blatant, explicit politics here. Is a Democrat or a Republican going to be president?* Show me one other case, ever, that was so outrageously political as this one. If any reader asks a fine-feathered conservative friend of theirs to cite such a case for them, I would advise them to bring a pair of earmuffs along, because the silence will be deafening. There has never been a case in U.S. Supreme Court history that even remotely approaches this one in being so politically motivated.

*Writing in *The Weekly Standard* on December 25, 2000, conservative columnist Michael S. Greve from the American Enterprise Institute, a conservative think tank, says that "It would be silly to deny that partisan considerations influenced ... the justices' rulings" (12-9-00 stay order and 12-12-00 decision in *Bush v. Gore*). But Greve is not critical of the conservative Justices, saying the ruling simply fell into a "pattern" of liberal and conservative Justices construing federalism in different ways. In an otherwise scholarly article, after acknowledging the "partisan" (i.e., political) ruling in *Bush v. Gore*, he immediately and seamlessly (as if he were unaware he was switching from talking about apples to oranges) segues into a discussion of the "two federalisms" that divide the Court, thereby failing to dichotomize between ideology and brass-knuckle politics.

Moreover, these previous, ideologically motivated decisions of the Court were never personally self-serving like this one. I'm, of course, being facetious here, but when, for instance, the Court ruled in *Roe v. Wade*, they weren't making abortions lawful because they wanted their wife or mistress to be able to have an abortion. Here, we know that Justice O'Connor wanted to retire, but she didn't want to do so if a Democrat was going to appoint her successor. And no one can seriously dispute that the other four conservative justices (Rehnquist [who, it is commonly known, is also thinking of retiring], Scalia, Thomas, and Kennedy) likewise wanted a Republican president to fill subsequent vacancies on the Court.

Finally, in almost all of these prior decisions of the Court that were driven by ideology (*Roe v. Wade* might be an exception), the Court also found a *valid legal basis* for their ruling. In *Bush v. Gore* there was none at all.

AMPLIFICATION SEVEN

SOME PEOPLE WHO have read the *Nation* article said to me words to this effect: "Mr. Bugliosi, since theft is a crime, why couldn't the five Justices be convicted of the theft of the presidency?"

Each crime has a *corpus delicti*, i.e., the body or elements of the crime. And unless each element is present, the crime has not been committed. For instance, one of the elements of the crime of burglary is that at the very moment the defendant entered the victim's residence he had the specific intent to steal. If he formed the intent after he entered and stole, let's say, a painting off the wall, he'd be guilty of the theft of the painting, but not burglary. With respect to the crime of theft, a representative statute is §484 of the California Penal Code, which provides that "every person who shall . . . steal . . . the *personal property* of another . . . is guilty of theft." In *United States v. Barlow*, 470 F.d 1245 (1972), the court said that the federal theft statute, 18 U.S.C. §641, "requires a wrongful taking and carrying away . . . of *personal property* of another. . . ." Hence, one of the elements of the *corpus delicti* of the crime of theft is that "personal property" be stolen. Although the courts have held that personal property can include intangibles, such as a bank check payable to the victim of the theft, or a ticket for a sporting event, the intangible has to have some monetary value. The theft of the presidency simply would not fall within the definition of theft, and to be a prosecutable crime would have to be the subject matter of a new Congressional enactment.

I say that the crime the Justices committed was not an actual crime since there was no specific law on the books prohibiting what they did. But with one Supreme Court Justice, the most important one, Chief Justice Rehnquist, he almost assuredly did commit an actual crime in 1986 in his confirmation hearings before the Senate for Chief Justice. The crime was perjury, and of the two basic types of perjury, Rehnquist's was the worst. Because the *Nation* article, and this book based thereon, makes the allegation that the five Supreme Court Justices are criminals, Rehnquist's crime of perjury, if true, becomes quite relevant. Before we discuss it, however, let's look at the first type of perjury and put it into the context of a criminal trial. The defendant, let's stipulate, did in fact commit the crime, but he takes the witness stand in front of the jury and denies under oath that he did. This form of self-defense, where no third party is hurt by it, is obviously anticipated and overlooked by prosecutors. We expect it. I mean, if the defendant was not going to deny having committed the crime, he would have pled guilty and there wouldn't have been any trial.

To prove how overlooked and essentially forgiven this type of self-defensive perjury is, in every case where a defendant has denied guilt from the witness stand and is subsequently convicted, the finding of guilt by the jury by definition is a concomitant finding that the jury believes the defendant committed perjury when he denied guilt under oath. Yet with the many thousands of defendants convicted every year throughout the land for various crimes, I have never heard or read of a case where, after the conviction, they were prosecuted for their perjury in denying the commission of the crime.

The above form of self-defensive perjury is precisely what took place in President Clinton's denial of having sexual relations with Monica Lewinsky. And that was a *civil* case. Although Clinton's right-wing enemies struggled mightily in his impeachment hearing to come up with a precedent, they were unable to come up with one single case ever of any man being prosecuted for perjury because of lying in a civil case about consensual sexual relations. Yet in divorce and child custody proceedings, for instance, this type of perjury has been committed hundreds of thousands of times throughout the years, and it's invariably overlooked. Though certainly not condoning or approving of these lies under oath, no prosecu-

tor would ever dream of prosecuting such a case, and no prosecutor in America, to my knowledge, ever has. Trying to go
after Clinton criminally for perjury in the Lewinsky case may
have been unprecedented in American legal history. The only
precedent anyone has ever brought to my attention is an
obscure 1913 case in rural Texas, but there the perjury was
very relevant since it was a paternity case and the man denied
having sex with the woman. With Clinton, the monstrous,
grotesque Ken Starr* pursued Clinton's lie under oath not
because it was relevant to any of the issues in the Paula
Jones case, but simply to prove he had lied so he could
destroy him. The judge at the president's deposition in the
Paula Jones case, Susan Weber Wright, had no business allowing the question about Lewinsky in the first
place, since the president's having sex with Lewinsky had no

ʸ If anyone wants to know why I say this, I would recommend that they read a
long interview with me in the December 1998 edition of *Penthouse* magazine, and
pages 135–136 of my book *No Island of Sanity*. Suffice it to say here that I never, ever
make a charge without offering support for it, and that Ken Starr is not a star, and he's
not a prosecutor. What he is, is a disgrace to prosecutors everywhere. As Manhattan
District Attorney Robert Morganthau says: "Ken Starr broke every rule in the book."
In fact, Starr went far beyond merely breaking rules. In my opinion, Starr is one of
the most reprehensible public figures we've ever been exposed to in America.

Quite apart from the gross wrong of President Clinton having sex in the Oval
Office, rightfully considered sacred turf by most Americans (it was said that
President Reagan had so much respect for the Oval Office that he wouldn't even
take off his suit coat while in the room, although his severest critics have responded that this was so only because he couldn't find the suit rack), Starr and his
defenders were fond of saying that the investigation of Clinton was not about sex
but about the president's unlawful attempt to cover it up. But that's putting the
cart way, way before the horse. Since not even Starr alleged that it was anything
but consensual sex between Clinton and Lewinsky, and therefore lawful activity,
no one had the right to criminally investigate this private relationship *in the first
place*. When you've done something—here, the president having sex with
Lewinsky—which, even though perfectly lawful, could destroy you if it becomes
known, does anyone, a court or anyone else, have the right to in effect say to you,
"Either you admit this thing that can destroy you, or, if you deny it, we're going to
prosecute you for perjury." In other words, either way you're going to be destroyed.
That, to me, sounds much more like totalitarianism than the free society we all
cherish. What I am saying is that the impropriety, the misconduct, the villainy, if
you will, is in the question, not the answer.

demonstrable relevance to the Paula Jones case in that Jones was claiming an unwanted sexual advance, and the president's relationship with Lewinsky, by all accounts, was consensual. Indeed, two weeks after Judge Wright improperly allowed the question, she realized her error and tried to rectify the situation by ruling that the president's testimony and Monica Lewinsky's affidavit in which they both denied having sex with each other would be inadmissible at the then-upcoming Paula Jones trial in Little Rock. But the damage had already been done. The monstrous, grotesque (I know I've already used these words) Ken Starr had his opening, and the rest, as they say, is history.

The second and by far the most serious type of perjury is not where one is merely denying doing something, the commission of which would result in affirmative harm to him if disclosed, but where one lies under oath to further his own ends, particularly where in the process he is seriously hurting a third party, such as accusing an innocent person of a crime. That type of perjury, if proved, normally does result in a criminal prosecution. It's this second type of perjury that the strong weight of the evidence shows Rehnquist committed.

After Rehnquist testified in his 1971 confirmation hearings before the Senate on his nomination to the Supreme Court, but before his appointment, *Newsweek* magazine got hold of and published (December 6, 1971) a 1952 memo from Rehnquist (who was then a law clerk for Justice Robert Jackson) to Jackson titled, "A Random Thought on the Segregation Cases." At the time, the Court was hearing arguments on the landmark case of *Brown v. Board of Education*. In the one-and-a-half-page memo, Rehnquist wrote that "I fully realize that it is an unpopular and unhumanitarian position for which I have been excoriated by liberal colleagues, but I think *Plessy v. Ferguson* (the 1896 case holding that the equal protection clause of the Fourteenth Amendment did not prohibit segregation as long as the public accommodations and facilities were equal for blacks and whites, enunciating the so-called "separate but equal doctrine") was right and should be reaffirmed." Knowing that such a position, in 1971, seventeen full years after *Brown v. Board of Education* repudiated the separate but equal doctrine, would sound the death knell for his appointment to the Court, Rehnquist immediately dispatched a letter to Senate Judiciary Committee chairman James Eastland in which he claimed the memo set forth Justice Jackson's views (Jackson had died in 1954), not his. "The memorandum was prepared by me at Justice Jackson's request," Rehnquist told Eastland. "It was intended as a rough draft of a statement of *his* views at the conference of Justices, rather than a statement of *my* views." *

Rehnquist said Jackson had asked him to assist him "in developing arguments which he might use" when he conferred with his fellow Justices in the pending *Brown v. Board of Education* case. The letter did not snuff out the flames of controversy ignited by the memo, but the Senate ultimately confirmed Rehnquist's nomination to the Court.

The issue came up again in 1986 when Rehnquist testified before the Senate in his confirmation hearings for Chief Justice. Now under oath, he once again maintained that the memo set forth Jackson's views, not his. Senator Ted Kennedy asked Rehnquist: "Do the 'I's' [in the memo] refer to you?" "No, I do not think they do," Rehnquist answered.

* That Rehnquist himself did not have such views can easily be questioned. Not only has he been a deep-dyed conservative since his early years, but in 1967, as a lawyer in Phoenix, he opposed an integration plan for the Phoenix public schools. And in a March 3, 1985 interview, in the *New York Times*, he said (in a remarkable bit of candor in light of the always potentially incendiary 1952 memo) that although he accepts *Brown v. Board of Education* as the law, "I think there was a perfectly reasonable argument the other way."

"You maintain the 'I's' refer, then, to Justice Jackson?" Kennedy pressed on. "Yes. Obviously something for him to say," Rehnquist replied.

Did Rehnquist commit perjury in 1986? At the time in 1971 that Rehnquist's appointment to the Court was in jeopardy because of the 1952 pro-*Plessy* memo, his fellow law clerk back in 1952, Donald Cronson, by now a Mobil Oil executive based in London, tried to come to his defense, sending Rehnquist a cable that was placed in the *Congressional Record*. The cable said that Jackson had asked for two memos, pro and con on the segregation issue, and that the two of them had collaborated on both. Indeed, Cronson said, "it is probable that the [pro-*Plessy*] memorandum is more mine than yours." But there were problems for Rehnquist with Cronson's cable and his credibility. Number one, Cronson never suggested, as Rehnquist claimed, that the memo set forth Jackson's views. Secondly, if what Cronson said was true, what reason could Rehnquist have possibly had for not telling Eastland this in his letter? Surely a collaborative effort would have attenuated the case against him. Indeed, it would have virtually exonerated him since, per Cronson, the memo was more his than Rehnquist's. Thirdly, the pro-*Plessy* memo had the initials "whr" for William H. Rehnquist at the bottom of it.

Cronson is virtually all Rehnquist has to support his position. (And his support, arguably, is no support at all, since nowhere did he say that Jackson wanted Rehnquist, as Rehnquist claimed, to set forth Jackson's views.) On the other side is not only common sense but very persuasive evidence that Rehnquist lied in his 1971 letter and committed perjury in his 1986 testimony.

In the first place, the very language of the memo seems to clearly say that Rehnquist was writing his own beliefs, not Jackson's. If what Rehnquist said is true, that he was furnishing arguments and articulations for Jackson to use, the pronoun "I" would be completely inappropriate. Words like "You might argue" or "The point could be made" would make much more sense and be far more normal. Moreover, if the purpose of the memo was for Jackson's use with his colleagues on the Court, why would Rehnquist write "I have been excoriated by liberal colleagues"? Jackson was a moderate Democrat, not an ultra-conservative Republican like Rehnquist, and he had no history on the Court of wanting to perpetuate an inherently racist philosophy.* So why would his fellow Justices be "excoriating" him? For what? Even if we were to assume that Jackson had been a judicial racist and his colleagues had been excoriating him, why would Rehnquist be telling Jackson to inform his colleagues that they had been excoriating him for his views? Wouldn't they already know what they allegedly had been doing? Rehnquist's position is irrational on its face.

Richard Kluger, author of *Simple Justice, The History of Brown v. Board of Education and Black America's Struggle for Equality*, the definitive 1976 book on the Brown case, says (page 608) that a far more plausible explanation is that "the 'I' in the memo is Rehnquist himself referring to the obloquy to which he may have been subjected by his fellow clerks. These same clerks discussed the segregation question over lunch quite regularly, and were almost unanimous in their belief that *Plessy* ought to be reversed, and were, for the most part, 'liberal.'" (Rehnquist, in the afore

---

*Although legal scholars agree that Jackson was opposed to *Plessy v. Ferguson*, a conflicting current in him was his respect for *stare decisis* (Latin for "let the decision stand"), the doctrine that when a court has laid down a principle of law as being applicable to certain facts, it should adhere to that principle in all future cases where the facts are substantially similar. E. Barrett Prettyman Jr., a law clerk for Jackson in the 1953 term, said, "In short, [Jackson] wanted the Court, in ending segregation, to admit that it was making new law for a new day." (Kluger, *Simple Justice*, page 609)

mentioned March 3, 1985, interview in the *New York Times*, said (p. 32) that he could "remember arguments we would get in as law clerks" at the Supreme Court in 1952–1953.) Kluger cites line and verse for Rehnquist being so conservative back then (and there is no evidence he has changed) that he was viewed as a "reactionary." Kluger goes on to say that at the December 13, 1952, court conference on the *Brown case*, there is "little" in Justice Harold Burton's notes on Jackson's remarks [that] resembles any of the thoughts attributed to him in the Rehnquist memo."

Additionally, Jackson was a justice of considerable talent and ability who was so highly regarded by his contemporaries that President Truman asked him to serve as chief prosecutor for the United States at the Nuremberg War Trials in 1945–1946. Rehnquist, not known at all for being linguistically facile, unfortunately is stuck with the wrong person for whom he had to write articulations. Jackson was known for the power of his oratory and his brilliant prose. That Jackson, thirteen years on the Court, would ask Rehnquist, his first-year law clerk, to write down what he should say to his colleagues, is again, silly on its face.

Did, in fact, Jackson ever ask his law clerks to write memos for him to be used in conference discussions with his colleagues? Professor Dennis J. Hutchinson of the University of Chicago is Justice Jackson's biographer. He told the *New York Times* in 1985 (March 3, 1985, "The Partisan: A Talk With Justice Rehnquist," p. 32) that after inspecting "every box, every detail" of the Justice's papers from the Court, he found no other instance during Jackson's thirteen years on the Court where, as Rehnquist insists happened, he asked a law clerk to prepare a memo for conference discussion summarizing the Justice's views. Hutchinson said Rehnquist's contention was "absurd."

And Elsie Douglas, Justice Jackson's longtime personal

secretary, told the *Washington Post* in 1971 that her reaction to Rehnquist's contention was "one of shock." Rehnquist, she said, had "smeared the reputation of a great justice . . . . I don't know anyone in the world who was more for equal protection of the laws than Mr. Jackson." Rehnquist's story, she said, was "incredible on its face." She added that Jackson never needed any clerk to formulate articulations or positions for him because he had a well-deserved reputation for spontaneous eloquence.

But there is further evidence that gives the lie to Rehnquist's position. In 1989, Bernard Schwartz, one of the foremost historians of the Supreme Court, discovered a 1954 draft of a concurring opinion in *Brown v. Board of Education* that was written by Jackson himself but never published. In it, Jackson writes: "I am convinced that present day conditions require us to strike from our books the doctrine of separate but equal facilities." This, of course, flatly and unequivocally contradicts and rebuts Rehnquist's testimony that Jackson asked him to articulate a pro-*Plessy*, racist position he could use with his colleagues. And Kluger, the author of *Simple Justice*, after evaluating all the evidence and documentation, concluded (page 609) that "[O]ne finds a preponderance of evidence to suggest that the memorandum in question—the one that threatened to deprive William Rehnquist of his place on the Supreme Court—was an accurate statement of his own views on segregation, not those of Robert Jackson."

Finally, on May 17, 1954, Jackson, hospitalized for a serious heart condition that took his life a few months later, left his hospital bed against his doctor's advice to join eight of his Supreme Court colleagues in the *Brown* decision overruling *Plessy v. Ferguson*. It strongly appears that Rehnquist committed perjury in 1986 and deliberately defamed the reputation and memory of a dead man who could not expose the lie from his grave, all to further his own career. (And this is the man who, in his ridiculous-looking striped robe, right-eously presided over the impeachment trial of President Clinton for lying under oath about a private, consensual sexual affair.) If Rehnquist made Justice Jackson turn over in his grave in 1971 and 1986, he made fifty million Americans toss in their sleep in 2000. I, for one, believe that Rehnquist should be making license plates, not sitting as the Chief Justice of the land. (See also, Donald E. Boles, *Rehnquist, The Early Years*, 1987; Jeffrey Rosen, *Rehnquist's Choice*, *The New Yorker*, January 11, 1999.)

AMPLIFICATION EIGHT

FOR MORE BACKROUND on O'Connor's remark, the *Wall Street Journal* article (December 12, 2000) referred to reads: "Justice O'Connor, a cancer survivor, has privately let it be known that, after 20 years on the high court, she wants to retire to her home state of Arizona. . . . At an election party at the Washington, D.C. home of Mary Ann Stoessel, widow of former Ambassador Walter Stoessel, the Justice's husband, John O'Connor, mentioned to others her desire to step down, according to three witnesses. But Mr. O'Connor said his wife would be reluctant to retire if a Democrat were in the White House and would choose her replacement. Justice O'Connor declined to comment [on the story]."

Newsweek, in its December 25 edition, wrote this about the same event: "Supreme Court Justice Sandra Day O'Connor and her husband, John, a Washington lawyer, have long been comfortable on the cocktail and charity ball circuit. So at an election-night party on November 7, surrounded for the most part by friends and familiar acquaintances, she let her guard drop for a moment when she heard the first critical returns shortly before 8 P.M. Sitting in her hostess's den, staring at a small black-and-white television set, she visibly started when CBS anchor Dan Rather called Florida for Al Gore. 'This is terrible,' she exclaimed. . . . Moments later, with an air of obvious disgust, she rose to get a plate of food, leaving it to her husband to explain her somewhat uncharacteristic outburst. John O'Connor said his wife was upset because they wanted to retire to Arizona, and a Gore win meant they'd have to wait another four years. O'Connor, the former Republican majority leader of the Arizona State Senate and a 1981 Ronald Reagan appointee, did not want a Democrat to name her successor. Two witnesses described this extraordinary scene to *Newsweek.* Responding through a spokeswoman at the high court, O'Connor had no comment."

Some have wondered why I made relatively light of O'Connor's not wanting to retire unless a Republican appointed her successor, and the connections of Thomas' wife and Scalia's two sons to the Bush campaign. The reason is that these things only go to the issue of whether any of the three Justices had a motive, or were more likely to act improperly, and are not strong evidence that they actually did. My article sets forth many very incriminating things that we *know* the justices did from which we can draw an inference of guilt, as opposed to the aforementioned matters that don't prove they did anything wrong at all, only that they were more likely to have.* Although laypeople think that motive is extremely important in a criminal case, motive to commit a crime hardly gets one to first base in most criminal prosecutions. It's only one of the starting points of the investigation. Irrespective of the presence of motive, the prosecutor still has to prove, *by solid evidence*, that the person or group he feels had a motive is the same person or group who committed the crime, a little fact that millions of Americans and virtually all conspiracy theorists ignore, for instance, in the assassination of President Kennedy. Taking the French proverb "*Qui en profite du crime en est coupable*" (Whoever profits from the crime is

---

*Motive should be distinguished from intent, two terms that are sometimes used interchangeably in the criminal law. Motive is the emotional urge which induces a person to say or do something. It is different from intent, for a person may intend to steal property or kill someone, and will be guilty of the theft or homicide irrespective of what his motive was (e.g., need, avarice, revenge, jealousy, etc.). While intent is an element of every serious crime, motive is never an element of the *corpus delicti* of any crime. Therefore, the prosecutor *never* has to prove motive. In fact, I've put people on death row without knowing for sure what their motive was—that is, why they did it. All I knew for sure was that they had put someone in his or her grave and had no right to do it.

However, even though the prosecution doesn't have any legal burden to prove motive, it is always better if it can, because just as the presence of motive (particularly where the defendant is the *only* one with a motive) is circumstantial evidence of guilt, the absence of motive is perhaps even stronger circumstantial evidence of innocence.

guilty of it) to heart, they are convinced that finding a motive is synonymous with finding the perpetrator. That if, in their mind, a particular group had a motive to kill Kennedy, that is enough to prove that said group did, in fact, do so, a non sequitur and broadjump of Olympian proportions. For example, Oliver Stone, in his movie, *JFK*, concluded that no fewer than ten separate groups or people had a motive to kill Kennedy, and this is why someone of his intelligence (but with his thinking cap turned very tightly to the off position) had, unbelievably, *all ten* involved in Kennedy's murder, the logical extension of such a childlike yet very prevalent mode of thinking.

With respect, for instance, to Justice O'Connor being perhaps predisposed to stealing the election for Bush, a courthouse wag could say, "Yeah, okay, she had the motive. But did she do it?" There is much evidence that she in fact did, and *that's* what I dwelled on in *The Nation* article, not the likelihood that she might.

AMPLIFICATION NINE

ACTUALLY, NOT A recount since the Votomatic machines, for whatever reason, never did detect the votes on these particular ballots. The manual count would be examining these ballots for the *first* time to see if, as provided for under §101.5614(5) of the Florida Election Code, there was a "clear indication of the intent of the voter." One example: The stylus punches a clear hole in the paper ballot, but the chad is still attached (hanging) by one or more of its four sides. In that situation the Votomatic machine frequently does not detect the vote, though the intent of the voter could not be any clearer.

In *Counting the Vote* by Ford Fassenden in the November 17, 2000 *New York Times*, he quotes industry officials who manufacture voting machines as saying that "the most precise way to count ballots is by hand." Palm Beach County Judge Charles E. Burton, the chairman of the canvassing board in Palm Beach during the election, was called as a witness for George Bush at the trial in Tallahassee before Judge Sanford Sauls, but acknowledged that one could discern the clear intent in hundreds of ballots that the Votomatic machines did not register as a vote. (Trial transcript, page 278, 12-2-00)

Twenty-one states in addition to Florida allow, by statute, for manual recounts. In fact, in what has to be considered one of the richest ironies in this case, although Republicans persistently chanted throughout the election controversy about how unreliable manual recounts are and they should not have been permitted in Florida, in 1997, their candidate, George W. Bush, signed into law a statute that not only provides for manual recounts, but goes further and specifically provides under Sec. 212.005(d) of the Texas Election Code that "A manual recount shall be conducted *in preference to* an electronic recount." As reported in the *New York Times* (November 23, 2000), "Texas large-ly follows the rationale . . . that the voter's intent is paramount and can be determined from incompletely punched ballots [so-called pregnant or dimpled chads]." Jeff Eubank, assistant to Texas Secretary of State Elton Bomer, a Bush appointee, said that "it has to be ascertainable or measurable intent of the voter."

EARLIER IN THE DAY, the conservative-leaning U.S. Court of Appeals for the Eleventh Circuit in Atlanta voted 8 to 4 to deny Bush's companion attempt to have that court stop the recount. Seven of the twelve members of the Court were appointed by Republican presidents, four by George W. Bush's father.

AMPLIFICATION ELEVEN

OBVIOUSLY, TO MAKE the "irreparable harm" argument, one has to show that there is *some impropriety* that will
cause said harm. *Here, there was none.* So the remarkable
Scalia, trying to pull a rabbit out of the hat when there was
no rabbit in the hat, said the undervotes were of "question-
able legality" (he offered no evidence of this other than his
bold declaration) and then made this preposterous argument:
"Count first and rule upon legality afterwards is not a recipe
for producing election results that have the public accept-
ance democratic stability requires." But Justice Scalia, you
failed to inform all of us how in the world anyone could
determine if these undervotes were valid or invalid if we did-
n't first look at them? Scalia's recipe to help his candidate,
Bush, was to *not* count or even look at these votes. Instead,
appoint Bush President, and then, *after* Bush's inauguration,
let the newspapers *look at* and *count* the votes. Scalia, in his
desperate effort to help Bush, took audacious illogic to previously unimaginable heights. As Tony Mauro wrote in *USA
Today* about Scalia's perverted reasoning: "Since when is not
knowing better than knowing?"

AMPLIFICATION TWELVE

THE COURT'S action was so wrong and so blatantly political that on January 13, 2001, over 500 law professors from around the country took out a full page ad in the *New York Times* denouncing the stay order. These professors now have a website on the internet and the list has grown to an astonishing 673 law professors.

The ad read: "By stopping the vote count in Florida, the United States Supreme Court used its power to act as political partisans, not judges of a court of law. We are professors of law at 137 American law schools, from every part of our country, of different political beliefs. But we all agree that when a bare majority of the U.S. Supreme Court halted the recount of ballots under Florida law, the five justices were acting as political proponents for candidate Bush, not as judges. It is not the job of a federal court to stop votes from being counted. By stopping the recount in the middle, the five justices acted to suppress the facts. Justice Scalia argued that the justices had to interfere even before the Supreme Court heard the Bush team's arguments because the recount might cast a cloud upon what [Bush] claims to be the legitimacy of his election. In other words, the conservative justices moved to avoid the threat that Americans might learn that in the recount, Gore got more votes than Bush. This is presumably irreparable harm because if the recount proceeded and the truth once became known, it would never again be possible to completely obscure the facts. But it is not the job of the courts to polish the image of legitimacy of the Bush presidency by preventing disturbing facts from being confirmed. Suppressing the facts to make the Bush government seem more legitimate is the job of propagandists, not judges. By taking power from the voters, the Supreme Court has tarnished its own legitimacy. As teachers whose lives have been dedicated to the rule of law, we protest."

To my knowledge, there has been no advertisement or website by conservative law professors supporting the stay order.

THE DISGRACED FIVE Supreme Court Justices have clearly been embarrassed by this terrible flip-flop on the equal protection issue, and although they won't deign to discuss the legal rationale for their ruling with the hoi polloi, they have made sure that a defense for their ruling has gotten out there for the media to pick up.

In a surprisingly soft and accommodating article by Linda Greenhouse in the *New York Times* on February 20 (an article that doesn't mention the Florida Supreme Court's ruling on the evening of December 11, which most likely was responsible for the equal protection flip-flop more than anything else [see discussion near the end of the Summary]). Greenhouse, a reporter who previously wrote some excellent articles on the case and covers the U.S. Supreme Court for the *New York Times*, writes that the word from her sources (not the Justices themselves, of course, but presumably those they want to carry the water for them) is that the Justices' decision to delete the equal-protection issue from the first Bush appeal reflected a conclusion "that the question was not yet ripe for review rather than that it was uninteresting or irrelevant." The reason it wasn't ripe? The Bush side had a companion case alleging the same equal protection violation in the U.S. Court of Appeals for the Eleventh Circuit in Atlanta, and that case was "still pending." However, Erwin Chemerinsky of U.S.C. Law School in Los Angeles, who has been a constitutional law professor for twenty-one years, told me that "the fact the equal protection argument was pending in a lower court would in no way legally preclude the Supreme Court from granting certiorari in this case." Chemerinsky went on to say that he believes the reason why the high court denied certiorari on the equal protection argument is that it was "a very weak" argument. Nearly all legal scholars he knows, he says, agree with this assessment.*

It should be further noted on this point that since the U.S. Supreme Court, by granting Bush's writ of certiorari (i.e., agreeing to hear his appeal) on November 24, was thereby saying that it intended to intervene and assert its jurisdiction over the presidential election. Therefore, since time was of the essence, if they thought the equal protection clause argument had any real merit, common sense tells one that it would be highly unlikely for the Court to allow, and wait for, a lower court in Atlanta to deal with the equal protection issue on its own timetable.

The five Justices know that it frequently takes a long time for the truth to catch up with a lie, and also know that no more than one out of a thousand readers will check the lie out or even have any ready access to the truth. Greenhouse also carries out—inadvertently, I'm sure—the further propaganda of the five Justices when she writes that when the equal protection issue came before the court the second time, "it had evolved into something *new*. The question was no longer whether it was constitutional to recount votes in some counties and not others, but whether it was constitutional to count votes by standards that differed from county to county." But this simply is not true. Bush also raised this issue on November 22, the first time he appealed to the Supreme Court. In its equal protection argument to the high court, the Bush brief argued that there were "no established standards in place," and "a partially punched ballot, for

---

*For instance, Cass Sunstein, a University of Chicago law professor who considers himself an admirer of the Rehnquist court, told the *Los Angeles Times* that "as a matter of law," the equal protection argument adopted by the Court in its December 12 decision "is a real embarrassment."

example, may not be counted at all in most counties, might be counted as a vote in other counties, and in some counties it might be counted as a vote or not—depending on what set of ever changing rules the election officials happened to be applying at the time it is reviewed." This, Bush argued, "cannot withstand equal protection analysis."

AMPLIFICATION FOURTEEN

THE UNITED STATES Supreme Court ruling in *Bush v. Gore* handing the election to George Bush was really the second of two such decisions by the Court. I wrote about the first one in my book *No Island of Sanity, Paula Jones v. Bill Clinton: The Supreme Court on Trial* (Library of Contemporary Thought, Ballantine Publishing, 1998) the only book I'm aware of on the Supreme Court decision in the Paula Jones case. The case I made in my book for the proposition that the Supreme Court should have granted President Clinton's request to postpone the Jones trial until the end of his term was such that not only did the reviews in the *New York Times* and *Washington Post* agree, but to my knowledge not one conservative scholar *who has read* the book disagreed. The Supreme Court's ruling led to the Monica Lewinsky matter (President Clinton's denial, under oath, that he ever had sexual relations with Monica Lewinsky, took place in a deposition in Jones's lawsuit against the President), which grievously wounded the Clinton presidency to Al Gore's substantial detriment. Virtually everyone agrees that had it not been for the Lewinsky scandal, Gore would have won the election. In the *Jones* case, the Supreme Court displayed staggering judicial incompetence.

Briefly, my active interest in the Paula Jones case (*Clinton v. Jones*, 520 US 681 [1997]) began when I started to read about it and listen to discussions about it on television. I knew and remembered very clearly from my constitutional law course in law school that whenever a public interest is in conflict with a private one, the courts (not just the Supreme Court) *invariably* balance the interests to see which side is entitled to the most protection. I kept waiting to hear or read some reference to this in regard to the Paula Jones case, but there was absolutely no mention of it anywhere. Eventually, I ordered the opinion of the Court, written by Justice Stevens. Surely, it would be *there*, I told myself. But it was not. Next I ordered the legal brief to the Supreme Court submitted on August 8, 1996, by Robert Bennett, the president's lawyer, over nine months before the Court's decision on May 27, 1997. Incredibly, I found *just one sentence* in Bennett's entire forty-seven-page brief where balancing of interests was even mentioned, and that was secreted way back on page forty. Bennett's whole argument was based on separation of powers, an elegant but very weak argument that the Court disposed of quickly and easily.

For the balancing-of-interests doctrine to come into play, the public interest, obviously, doesn't have to be one that involves the nation as a whole, as it did in the Jones case. Not even a state has to be involved. A city wants to build a highway, but currently there are homes on the land. Though people have a right to own property in America, the right of eminent domain prevails and the owners are forced to move out of their homes, whether they like it or not, after receiving fair compensation for their property. In Los Angeles, a court order (after balancing the interests) led to the authorities physically removing some recalcitrant elderly owners of small homes in the Chavez Ravine section of Los Angeles just to build Dodger Stadium.

The unanimous (9-0) decision of the Supreme Court in the Paula Jones case (if fifty million people say a foolish thing, it's still a foolish thing) was not only devoid of all common sense, but violated the Court's own fundamental legal principles. Whenever the court, *any* court in the land, is confronted with two valid but conflicting interests—in this case, Paula Jones's interest in having her case brought to trial immediately (i.e., during the president's term) and the right of Americans to have a full-time president, one that can carry out his duties running the country without the enormous distraction of a private lawsuit—the court *must*, as it had routinely been doing (I cite many cases in

No Island) for over two centuries, balance the interests to
see which interest is the most important and should prevail.

For whatever reason, the Court curiously, one could
almost say mysteriously, did not balance the interests in the
Paula Jones case. If they had, what conceivable argument
under the moon could possibly be made for the proposition
that Paula Jones's individual right to proceed to trial, right
in the middle of the president's term, outweighed and was
more important than the right of 270 million Americans to
have their president be undiverted and undistracted in the
performance of his duties? Whether we like a particular
president or not, he works every day on national and international problems that affect all of our lives.

There was another separate and independent public
interest involved in the *Jones* case. An American president
represents this nation and its image in the world community more than anyone else by far. Anything that diminishes
him automatically diminishes our country in the eyes of the
world. (This is a public interest that the president's lawyers
failed to argue to the Supreme Court or even vaguely allude
to. It alone, and quite apart from the public interest that
the president be able to perform his duties undiverted by
private lawsuits, was another very substantial public interest that infinitely outweighed the right of Paula Jones to
have her lawsuit tried immediately.) Here we had a situation, for instance, where Paula Jones would be testifying in
Little Rock in front of the world press about allegedly "dis-
tinguishing characteristics" in the president's genital area.
Can anyone concerned about the stature and dignity of the
office of the presidency not be concerned about this? Even
without a trial, we had already become the laughingstock of
nations around the world. But none of this mattered, however, to the United States Supreme Court. In their mind,
Paula Jones's *individual* right to go to trial *right now* took

precedence over all other considerations affecting this nation and its millions of citizens.

What happened here is that the Supreme Court, in effect, held that Paula Jones had an *absolute* right to go to trial without any delay, essentially ignoring the public interest. They concerned themselves only with her rights. The Court said that a continuance of the trial till the end of the president's term "takes no account whatever of the respondents [Jones's] interest in bringing this case to trial . . . Like every other citizen . . . respondent has a right to an orderly disposition of her claims."* But of course, no right in our society is absolute, even our most cherished right, freedom of speech, when it impinges on other, more important rights. For instance, the law of libel is an exception to freedom of speech. And we all remember Justice Oliver Wendell Holmes Jr.'s observation in *Schenck v. United States*, 249 U.S. 47 (1919), that freedom of speech does not allow someone to shout fire in a crowded theater when there is no fire. In fact, even the right to live is not absolute. We execute people all the time in America.

Unlike in *Bush v. Gore*, where a great number of legal experts criticized the ruling, prior to *No Island* I personally am not aware of any magazine article (there never were any books), newspaper column, or even talking-heads who said the Court was wrong in its ruling in the Jones case. To the contrary, as writer Jeffrey Toobin wrote in a November 3, 1997, article in *The New Yorker*, the Court's opinion "drew wide praise for reflecting the bedrock American principle

---

*If some future plaintiff sues a president for a breach of contract on a very complex real estate transaction involving a great number of witnesses and thousands upon thousands of pages of documents in Sheboygan, Wisconsin, and the trial is expected to last six months, the president should go to Sheboygan for six months for the trial in the middle of his term. It certainly makes good sense to me.

that no one is above the law." Indeed, even those who did not affirmatively praise the decision, and lamented the ruling, nevertheless said that the Court did what it had to do. I give many quotes in *No Island* to this effect. Here are a few representative ones. An editorial in the *National Law Journal* (June 9, 1997) said that the Supreme Court's decision "holds dangers for the U.S. presidency and for the U.S. political system itself," but concluded that "[t]he court's ruling in *Jones v. Clinton* makes . . . legal sense." The editorial board of the *New Jersey Law Journal* (June 23, 1997) said: "The Supreme Court's rejection of the president's separation of powers argument [again, the president's lawyers did not rely on the balancing of interests argument] for immunity from private lawsuits may have been proper. . . . The court may not have had any choice but to state this very democratic and republican sentiment." Walter Shapiro, political columnist for *U.S.A. Today*, wrote that what the Court ruling portended for the president "should make us all feel a little embarrassed to be Americans," and "no president deserves the humiliation of this lawsuit." But he added, "I have no quarrel with the Supreme Court decision. The principle that no one, not even a sitting president, should be above the law is embedded in our legal system." After first "lamenting" the fact that the president would be forced to go to trial by the Court's ruling, Harvard Law School's Laurence Tribe wrote in *George* magazine (September, 1997 edition) that he nonetheless "agreed with the court's ultimate conclusion. . . . It is a basic axiom of our government that no one is above the law, not even the president."

It has to be noted that in an earlier June 13, 1994, appearance by Tribe on *Nightline* (before the decision of the Supreme Court), after host Ted Koppel introduced frequent guest Tribe by saying, "He favors delaying the case against the president until he's out of office," Tribe proceeded to sound like me in my 1998 book *No Island*. Some excerpts:

"It's absolutely vital that the president not be burdened, any president not be burdened, by these kinds of distractions in office"; "Under our constitutional system, the task of balancing the plaintiff's need for an immediate day in court [against] the debilitation on the executive is a task that properly falls to the judicial branch." What should the result of that balancing be in this case? "I think, in a case like this . . . the appropriate adjustment is temporary delay"; "It's the office of the presidency which needs to be protected, not Nixon, Clinton, not Reagan, not Bush"; "There's no pressing urgency that demands having a sitting president respond to a suit for damages of this sort."

What new thing Professor Tribe learned about constitutional law between his appearance on *Nightline* before the Court's ruling in the *Jones* case and his article in *George* after it, I can't imagine.

The biggest misconception about the Paula Jones case, by far, was that the Court ruled the way it did because "no one is above the law, not even the president." But even the Supreme Court itself said in its decision that the president was not asserting that he was above the law—that is, seeking absolute immunity. He was merely asking for a continuance. ("Petitioner [the president] . . . does not contend that the occupant of the Office of the President is 'above the law' in the sense that his conduct is entirely immune from judicial scrutiny. The President argues merely for a postponement of the judicial proceedings.") But the incredible media, a group that can always be counted upon to do a minimum of thinking (there are, of course, some notable exceptions), allowed this simple request by Clinton for a postponement of the trial to the end of his term to metamorphose into the issue of whether he was above the law. The media nitwits were constantly yammering "He's not above the law, He's not above the law," and that became the cliché for the average person on the street as well as the talking heads on television. Actually, under certain circumstances, thousands of people in our society are literally above the law. Judges, prosecutors, legislators, for example, have absolute immunity from all *civil*—but not criminal—lawsuits (and let's not forget that the Jones case was only a civil lawsuit) arising out of their official duties, even if, the courts have held, the alleged conduct was "malicious and corrupt." In other words, the plaintiff's rights are permanently extinguished. Paula Jones's rights would not have been. The question was not *whether* Jones should have her day in court, but *when*.

Most analogous to Paula Jones's lawsuit against the president (because of the rationale given for the deferral of lawsuits thereunder) is the *Soldiers' and Sailors' Civil Relief Act of 1940*, 50 U.S.C. App. Sections 501—25, which expressly tolls (stays, suspends) civil claims against military personnel, if they so request, during the course of their active duty. Why? Section 510 provides that "provision is made to suspend enforcement of civil liabilities . . . of persons in the military service of the United States in order to enable such persons to *devote their entire energy to the defense needs of the nation*." The statute goes on to say that this means "the temporary suspension of legal proceedings." As the Court said in *Slove v. Strohm*, 236 N.E. 2nd 326 (1968), "The purpose of the *Soldier's' and Sailors' Civil Relief Act* is to permit members of the armed forces to *devote their full attention* to the defense of the country." And in *Blazejowski v. Stadnicki*, 58 N.E., 2nd 164 (1944), the Court said, "The purpose of the act was to ensure to those in the armed services a state of mind relatively at peace so far as the cares and burdens of civil litigation is concerned."

So even during peacetime, a buck private going through basic training at Fort Benning, Georgia, whose principal challenge is to learn how to assemble and disassemble an M-16 rifle, is legally entitled to a postponement of any civil action against him so that he can devote all his energy and attention to his duties, but the president of the United States, who has the most important and demanding job on earth, is not. Is this sense, or nonsense? What previously recognized form of logic would allow this?*

Why did the Court make the enormous blunder that it did in the *Jones* case? I discuss several possibilities in *No Island*. One of them is that if one starts out with an erroneous premise, everything that follows makes a heck of a lot of sense. The only problem is that it's wrong. And in the *Jones* case, Justice Stevens, who wrote the Court's opinion, said that Bill Clinton was just someone who "happens to be the President." In other words, just some person from Hope, Arkansas, who was presently residing with his family at 1600 Pennsylvania Avenue in Washington, D.C. So although the president has the power to treat all of *us* completely differently than anyone else does—send us to war, pardon criminals, appoint people to the Supreme Court—

*What the president was seeking was *temporary* immunity, not absolute immunity, from a civil lawsuit. Could the argument be made that the only reason the Supreme Court in the *Jones* case did not grant the president the relief he sought simply was that Congress had not enacted any statute expressly providing him (like military personnel) with such relief? The answer is no. As the Supreme Court itself said in *Nixon v. Fitzgerald*, 457 U.S.731 (1982) [not to be confused with *U.S. v. Nixon*, 418 U.S. 683 (1974), the Watergate case], where it granted absolute immunity to presidents for lawsuits arising out of their official acts, "a specific *textual* (that is, *statutory*) basis has *not* been considered a prerequisite to the recognition of immunity." Nor does there have to be any *constitutional* basis for immunity. In *Butz v. Economou*, 438 U.S. 478(1978), the Supreme Court held that the secretary of agriculture and his assistants were entitled to absolute immunity from job-related civil lawsuits, noting that "the doctrine of official immunity . . . [is] not constitutionally grounded." If you don't need a constitutional basis for absolute immunity, you certainly don't need it for the lesser temporary immunity the president was seeking. Does it make any difference that, as opposed to the absolute immunity cases, unofficial conduct of the president was involved in the Paula Jones case? I don't see why. Unofficial conduct in no way eliminates the need to balance the public against the private interest. If, as we know, unofficial conduct of military personnel, even buck privates, doesn't eliminate the need to balance the interests, why should it with the president of the United States?

we should treat *him* like he's no different than the person
next door. In other words, just someone "who happens to be
the president."

But the thing is, the fact that he "happens to be the president" is just what requires that we *do* treat him differently.
Because of his importance to the nation, whenever the president leaves the White House, a large medical van with a doctor and staff—almost a miniature hospital, with the very lat-
est in life-saving equipment—follows behind the presidential
limousine. Never far from the president when he leaves the
White House is an inconspicuous and unknown military
aide who carries a little black briefcase they call the "foot-
ball" that contains, for the president's use only, the tech-
nology and codes to launch nuclear weapons that can
incinerate a hostile nation within minutes. An entire federal agency, the Secret Service, with several thousand
employees, is in existence in large part to protect the president. Why, if he's not more special and important to the
republic than you or I, Justice Stevens, is this so? So we
want to protect the president's physical body like no other
person's body in this land of ours, but according to you and
your colleagues, we shouldn't have any desire to protect and
shield, in any way at all, his mind, which controls his body.
I see. Who am I to quarrel with such powerful logic as this?

I wrote in *No Island* (at a point in time when the case was
scheduled to be tried in Little Rock, and before it was settled
out of court by Clinton) that "I can easily foresee the trial
igniting such a vast and deafening media explosion by the
world press, and the situation getting so out of hand because
of sensational allegations and *new and damaging revelations*
that the president has to respond to, that he might become
more than substantially distracted by the lawsuit. Rather, he
will be . . . consumed by his political survival." Reviewing *No
Island* in *U.S.A. Today*, Tony Mauro wrote: "Six days before
Monica Lewinsky became a household name, famed Los

Angeles lawyer Vincent Bugliosi turned in a book manuscript that foresaw it all." I'm not the brightest person in the world, but a two-year-old should have been able to see the terribly dangerous situation and precedent the Court was establishing by its decision.

If anyone has any lingering doubts whether the Supreme Court in the *Jones* case made an erroneous ruling, I offer much more support for this conclusion in the text of *No Island*. The relevance of the *Jones* case to *Bush v. Gore* is that even if one were to reject all the evidence that I believe points irresistibly to the conclusion that the five Justices criminally and deliberately stole the election for Bush, that should not prevent them from still conceding that at a minimum the Court (as in the *Jones* case) ruled incorrectly when it concluded there was a violation of the equal protection clause of the Fourteenth Amendment. For those who have the mistaken notion that the Supreme Court, being the highest court in the land, simply doesn't make serious mistakes, I say that not only does the Jones case prove the opposite of that proposition, but the Court itself would not agree with that assessment. Every time the court overrules a previous decision of theirs, they are in effect saying they were wrong the first time around. A few illustrative cases. *O'Malley v. Woodrough*, 307 U.S. 207 (1939), overruled *Miles v. Graham*, 268 U.S. 501 (1925), as to the constitutionality of taxation of the salaries of federal judges; *United States v. Darby*, 312 U.S. 100 (1941), overruled *Hammer v. Dagenhart*, 247 U.S. 251 (1918), as to Congressional power over labor in the manufacture of goods; in fact, as recently as December 10, 1997, the U.S. Supreme Court, in *Hudson v. U.S.*, 522 US 93, ruled that a criminal prosecution arising out of conduct for which there had already been a civil fine did not violate the double jeopardy clause of the Fifth Amendment, thus overruling their previous decision in *United States v. Halper*, 490 U.S. 435

(1989). The *Halper* decision, by the way, was, like the Paula Jones case, a unanimous decision of the Court. Chief Justice Rehnquist, who wrote the *Hudson* opinion and, it should be noted, was also chief justice at the time of the *Halper* decision, said: "We believe *Halper's* deviation from longstanding double jeopardy principles was ill-considered." In other words, the Supreme Court, in *Hudson*, admitted that it goofed, made a mistake, was wrong, in *Halper*.

I view the Supreme Court in the *Jones* case like a driver who causes a massive accident on the freeway, and then drives on, looking at the pileup in the rear view mirror.

AMPLIFICATION FIFTEEN

MANY CONSERVATIVES HAVE referred to the Supreme Court decision as a 7-2, not a 5-4 decision, because Justices Souter and Breyer also found problems with the lack of a uniform standard. But this is hogwash. The decision was 5-4. Though Souter and Breyer did find equal protection problems, they in no way voted to reverse the Florida Supreme Court's December 8 decision mandating a state-wide recount. They voted to simply remand the case back to the Florida Supreme Court with instructions to establish a uniform standard and then continue with the recounting of undervotes.

AMPLIFICATION SIXTEEN

IN FACT, L. KINVIN WROTH, dean of the Vermont Law School and an expert on the Electoral College, said that "a recount could have gone on right up to the last day of Congress' joint session" on January 6, when the votes of the College were counted in Congress.

AMPLIFICATION SEVENTEEN

IN THE REAL world, there isn't even any need for a specific statutory provision authorizing extensions (or "continuances" as they are usually referred to by lawyers and judges) of time beyond a mandatory or "shall" date. Common sense and conventional notions of fairness and expediency dictate that good or just cause is a basis for an extension of time. Our system of justice would be unbelievably harsh, robotic, and yes, ineffective, without this necessary concession. But actually, the U.S. Supreme Court itself has memorialized this fact of life in its own published Rules. For instance, Rule 13(1) of the Court provides that an appeal to the Court to review a lower court judgment (called a petition for a writ of certiorari) *must* be filed with the clerk of the Court "within 90 days after entry of the judgment" in the lower court. But Rule 13(5) says that "*For good cause*, a Justice (just one, mind you, not a majority of five) may *extend* the time to file a petition for a writ of certiorari for a period not exceeding 60 days." (In fact, Section 2101(c) of Title 28 of the United States Code expressly provides this.) So these five conservative Justices, in rules that they themselves have promulgated, see no problem at all with granting up to a 60-day extension of time to a litigant appealing to them if he can show good cause, but they found it simply impossible to grant a one or two day extension of a date (one that wasn't even mandatory) to determine who the rightful winner of a presidential election is. If any reader doesn't think this is criminal, then I would ask them if they only think crimes can be committed with guns and knives.

Perhaps the principal cornerstone for Governor Bush's petition (to have the Florida Supreme Court's order granting an extension of time for the counting of the undervotes set aside) was the argument that such an extension violated Title 3 of the United States Code, Section 5. Let's see how Title 3 handles mandatory "shall" dates, dates that the Republicans genuflected before as being sacrosanct, sacred, and inviolable. Section 1 of Title 3 provides that "the electors of President and Vice President *shall* be appointed, in each state, on the Tuesday next after the first Monday in November." What happens if, for whatever reason, a state has failed to appoint electors "on the day prescribed by law"? No problem. Section 2 of Title 3 says "the electors may be appointed on a *subsequent* day in such a manner as the legislatures of such state may direct." So much for mandatory, shall dates under Title 3.

In fact, in the United States Supreme Court's own opinion on December 12 reversing the Florida Supreme Court and relying heavily on the position that Gore had run out of time, a time, apparently, that simply could not be extended under any circumstances, they unwittingly, by their very own words in another part of their opinion, betrayed and tattled on what they knew to be the truth but hid from others. The November 14 deadline in Florida supposedly was a statutory deadline for the return of vote counts to the Secretary of State. Yet the *per curiam* opinion reads: "The Secretary [of State] declined to waive the November 14 deadline imposed by statute." Say again? Whether the court majority realized it or not, what their words can only reasonably mean is that the statutory date was only a deadline and only mandatory if the authorities (i.e., Katherine Harris, the Secretary of State) wanted it to be. If they didn't, *voila*, it ceased to be mandatory. If the Supreme Court truly believed the November 14 date was a real deadline, then I suggest that the language it used was wholly inappropriate. The only proper and accurate language would have been that "the Secretary of State did what she was compelled, by law, to do—not allow submissions of returns beyond the statutory deadline of November 14."

On this very same point, the judge of the Circuit Court of the Second Judicial District in Leon County issued an order on November 14 which reads in part: "The county canvassing boards are, indeed, mandated to certify and file their returns with the Secretary of State by 5:00 P.M. today, November 14, 2000. There is nothing, however, to prevent the County Canvassing Boards from filing with the Secretary of State further returns after completing a manual recount. . . . Just as the County Canvassing Boards have the authority to exercise discretion in determining whether a manual recount should be done, the Secretary of State has the authority to exercise her discretion in reviewing that decision, considering all attendant facts and circumstances, and decide whether to include or ignore the late filed returns in certifying the election results and declaring the winner." In other words, the November 14 date was mandatory, but it was not mandatory.

So what's all this nonsense and tommyrot about mandatory deadlines and the U.S. Supreme Court ruling the way it did because there were only two hours left in the day on December 12, another *alleged* statutory deadline? These so-called deadlines are clearly only deadlines when they suit the purpose of the person or group that is in a position to decide whether they are mandatory.

AMPLIFICATION EIGHTEEN

AFTER THE PUBLICATION of the *Nation* article, I spoke to Erwin Chemerinsky, constitutional law professor at the University of Southern California, and asked him if he knew of any other case in United States Supreme Court history where the Court had limited its ruling to the case in front of it. "No, I don't," Chemerinsky said, *"Bush v. Gore* is a first. I don't believe any prior Supreme Court has ever done something like this before."

AMPLIFICATION NINETEEN

SOMEWHAT IRONICALLY, President George W. Bush's father, George Bush, was one of the most qualified men, in terms of his background, ever to become president. The elder Bush, in addition to being a genuine American war hero, was a U.S. Congressman from Texas, national chairman of the Republican National Committee, ambassador to China, Director of the CIA, and served eight years as vice-president of the United States. Backgrounds don't come too much better than this.

AMPLIFICATION TWENTY

TREASON IS THE only crime whose definition appears in the U.S. Constitution: "Treason against the United States shall consist only in levying War against them, or adhering to their Enemies, giving them Aid and Comfort . . ." (Art. 3, §3, cl.1) With respect to the second type of treason, the courts have defined "enemy" as a "foreign power," and the aid and comfort to the foreign country has to take place while the U.S. is "in a state of open hostility" with the other country, i.e., while we're at war. *Stephan v. United States*, 133 F.2d87, 94 (1943); see also *Cramer v. United States*, 325 U.S. 1, 3, 28-29 (1945). While the conduct of the five conservative Justices doesn't fall within the strict language of treason, the essence of treason, clearly, is an American citizen (which each of the Justices is) doing grave and unjustifiable damage to this nation, which the Justices surely did by stealing the office of the presidency for the candidate of their choice. How much of a distinction is there between helping an enemy hurt us, and hurting us yourself, whether at peace or war?

People have asked me about the possibility of impeachment (by the House of Representatives under Article 2, §4 of the U.S. Constitution) and eventual removal from office of these five Justices. It's only a theoretical, not a real possibility, since a two-thirds vote of the Senate would be necessary to convict. This would require all fifty Democratic senators and seventeen Republican senators to vote for conviction. Not only wouldn't all fifty Democratic senators so vote, but I doubt that even one, much less seventeen Republican senators would. (Only one Supreme Court Justice, Samuel Chase, in 1804, was impeached by the House of Representatives, but he was acquitted in the Senate after a two month trial.) It should be pointed out, however, that although the general belief is that Supreme Court appointments are "lifetime appointments," this is only essentially, not literally, true. Article 3, §1 of the United States Constitution provides that Supreme Court Justices "shall hold their offices *during good behavior*." The five Justices in *Bush v. Gore* certainly were on good behavior, weren't they?

PART

3

SUMMARY

A Brief History of the Legal Proceedings
Leading up to the December 12, 2000,
Ruling of the U.S. Supreme Court in *Bush v. Gore*

INASMUCH AS THE Florida election controversy ended up generating close to six thousand pages in legal documents (briefs, motions, opinions, etc.), a plethora of lawsuits, much misinformation, and many misconceptions by everyday Americans, a brief history of the controversy, without delving too far into its sinuous complexities, would seem to be in order; keeping in mind throughout that ultimately the *per curiam*, majority opinion of the U.S. Supreme Court *only* found an Equal Protection Clause violation by the Florida Supreme Court, not violations of Art. 2 (of the federal constitution) or Title 3 (of the U.S. Code).

It all started, of course, on Tuesday, November 7, 2000, when the state of Florida, along with the rest of the country, voted in the election for president of the United States. The Florida Division of Elections reported the following day that George W. Bush, the Republican candidate, had received 2,909,135 votes and Albert Gore Jr., the Democratic candidate, had received 2,907,351 votes, giving Bush a plurality of 1,784 votes. Because the overall difference in the total votes cast for each candidate was less than one-half of one percent of the total votes cast for president, an automatic machine recount was conducted pursuant to §102.141(4) of the Florida Election Code. The recount, conducted on November 8 and 9, resulted in Bush's plurality being reduced to only 327 votes.

In light of the closeness of the election, on November 9, the Florida Democratic Executive Committee (not the Gore campaign)—under §102.166 of the Florida Election Code, the "protest" section of the Code—requested that manual (hand) recounts (authorized under §102.166(4)(c) of the code) be conducted in Broward, Palm Beach, Miami-Dade, and Volusia Counties, all counties that voted for Gore. Asking for a manual recount in just a few counties, as opposed to the whole state, is the rule, not the exception. (Bush did not request at that time, or at any subsequent time, a manual recount in any Florida county.) Under §102.166(4)(d) of the code, before there is a recount there must first be a sample manual recount of "at least one percent of the total votes cast" in the subject counties. Sections 102.166(5) and 102.166(5)(c) of the code provide that if the sample recount "indicates an error in the vote tabulation which could affect the outcome of the election," the county canvassing boards are authorized to "manually recount all the ballots" in the county.

When the sample recount in this case—commenced on November 11 and finished on November 12—showed that Gore picked up several net votes that were not detected by the Votomatic machines (in Broward, Palm Beach and Miami-Dade) and the optical scanners (in Volusia) but were discernible upon manual examination (e.g., nineteen net votes in Palm Beach County), all four counties decided (though two, Broward and Miami-Dade, not immediately) to conduct a full manual recount of all the votes in their respective counties. Palm Beach wanted to start immediately on the 12th but couldn't. As Theresa LePore, the supervisor of elections for Palm Beach County told me, "It took a few days just to set up the logistics for the manual recount, such as getting all the vote counters, a location large enough to handle the recount (they ended up in the Palm Beach County Emergency Operations Center, a hurricane bunker), providing for security, et cetera."

The immediate problem facing the four counties on November 12, of course, was that with literally hundreds of thousands of votes that had to be hand counted (588,007 ballots in Broward County, 179,661 in Volusia, 462,888 in Palm Beach, and 654,044 in Miami-Dade), how could the counties possibly get their amended returns in by November 14 (under sections 102.111 and 102.112 of the Florida Elections Code, county returns had to be "received by the Department of State by 5:00 P.M. of the seventh day following an election," that is, November 14)? As Ms. LePore said, "I hadn't even completed the logistics for the manual recount by the fourteenth." Judge Charles E. Burton, the chairman of the Palm Beach County canvassing board, added that "none of the three larger counties [Broward, Palm Beach and Miami Dade] could have possibly finished their manual recount by the November 14 deadline." However, the circuit court (a trial court in Florida) in Leon County in Tallahassee ruled on November 14 that the deadline was mandatory, but said that counties could still conduct their manual recount beyond that date and the secretary of state could exercise her discretion in determining whether or not to accept amended returns received by her *after* November 14. In other words, the date was mandatory, but it really wasn't. It was all up to the secretary of state, Katherine Harris.

Harris issued a directive late that same day, November 14, requiring all counties that intended to submit amended late returns (Broward, Palm Beach and Miami Dade) to inform her of this fact, as well as the reasons for the late returns, by the following day, November 15. The three counties, none of which had commenced their manual

recount yet, did so, and on November 15 the obdurate
Harris gave each of their explanations for a late filing an F,
ruling that only a showing of voter fraud, an act of God, or
a "mechanical malfunction of the voting tabulation system"
would qualify for an extension of time, and she found none
of those situations present. In other words, Harris had only
allowed the three counties between November 12 and
November 14 at 5:00 P.M. to hand count hundreds of thousands of votes, an obviously impossible task for large counties like Miami-Dade, Broward, and Palm Beach. (The
much smaller county of Volusia commenced its manual
recount earlier than the other three, on November 12, and
after a frenetic, yeoman effort, completed its manual
recount just five minutes before the 5:00 P.M. deadline on
November 14.) Harris asserted that after receiving the certified returns of the overseas absentee ballots (due no later
than November 17), she would certify the results of the
presidential election on Saturday, November 18, 2000.
(The Florida Supreme Court would later say that in view of
the "Florida election scheme," Harris's decision to reject
amended late returns filed after November 14 but before
November 18 constituted "a clear abuse of discretion,"
since she could not "certify the election prior to that date
[November 18]" anyway.)

The next day, November 16, the Florida Supreme Court,
on petition from the canvassing boards, issued a short
"interim order" that the ruling in the Leon County Circuit
Court providing that the south Florida counties could conduct a manual recount past the November 14 deadline was
"at present, binding legal authority," and thus "petitioners
are authorized to proceed with the manual recount." (The
Court didn't say whether Harris had to accept the late
returns.) Broward and Palm Beach counties commenced
their manual recounts that same day, November 16, but
Miami-Dade, never overly enthusiastic about conducting a

manual recount because of opposition in the heavily Republican Cuban-American community, took days "sorting" the nearly 700,000 ballots and didn't commence its recount until the morning of November 20.

Also, on November 16, the Florida Democratic Party and Al Gore* filed a motion in the Second Judicial District in Leon County seeking to compel the secretary of state to accept amended late returns. On November 17, the court denied relief and the Democratic Party and Gore appealed to the First District Court of Appeal, which instead of hearing the matter sent it straight up to the Florida Supreme Court. The Supreme Court, on November 17, enjoined the secretary of state from certifying the results of the Florida election until further order of the court.

After written briefs had been submitted and oral argument made to the Florida Supreme Court by both the Gore and Bush sides, on November 21 the Florida Supreme Court reversed the trial court's ruling that amended late returns could only be included in the secretary of state's certification if she chose, in her discretion, to permit it. Although there were solid statutory grounds for the Florida Supreme Court's ruling, there was an overriding principle the court also took into consideration, one that every court in the land that is interested in equity and justice would have likewise taken into consideration. Citing *Boardman v. Esteva*, 323 So. 2d 259 (Fla. 1975), the court said, "Twenty-five years ago, this court commented that the will of the people, not a hypertechnical reliance upon statutory provisions, should be our guiding principle in election cases." The court quoted the language from *Boardman*: "Ours is a government of, by and for the people. . . . The right to vote is the right to participate; it is also the

---

*When I say Al Gore and George Bush, or Bush or Gore hereafter, I obviously am not referring to Bush and Gore themselves, but to lawyers representing their respective campaigns and acting on their behalf.

right to speak, but more importantly the right to be heard. . . . By refusing to recognize an otherwise valid exercise of the right of a citizen to vote for the sake of sacred, unyielding adherence to statutory scripture, we would in effect nullify that right." (Thirteen years later, in *Chappell v. Martinez*, 536 So. 2d 1007 (1988), the Florida Supreme Court again said that "the electorate's effecting its will through its balloting, not the hypertechnical compliance with statutes, is the object of holding an election." The *Chappell* court approvingly cited language in *Boardman* that "there is no magic in the statutory requirements," and that if responsible election officials can ascertain that the votes are valid, "who can be heard to complain that the statute has not been literally and absolutely complied with?" George W. Bush, that's who. In *Chappell*, the results of the election were phoned in before the deadline, but the actual returns were not, as required, "received by the Department of State" until three days after the deadline.) The Florida Supreme Court added: "We consistently have adhered to the principle that the will of the people is the paramount consideration."

But the Florida Supreme Court went on to clearly point out that quite apart from this overriding principle, a simple and traditional interpretation by the court of existing Florida statutory law guided the court irresistibly to the same conclusion—that the amended late returns should be accepted. The court found two statutory ambiguities under Florida law to interpret and resolve. (This, at an absolute minimum, is its job. If it doesn't do this, it has no reason to exist. Things become problematic when appellate courts, including the U.S. Supreme Court, in effect, by their rulings, create new law. The Supreme Court has been doing this for years, and there seems to be no end in sight for this short of a constitutional amendment requiring that courts only interpret what the law is, not make new law, which is for our elected representatives to do.)

The first ambiguity was that the time frame for conducting a manual recount under §102.166(4) of the Florida Election Code was in conflict with the time frame for counties submitting their returns under §102.111 and §102.112. Under §102.166(4), a candidate can request a manual recount *at any point* prior to certification by the canvassing board of the county, and such action can lead to a full manual recount of all the votes in the county under §102.166(5)(c). The court said that "although the code sets no specific deadline by which a manual recount must be completed, logic dictates that the period of time required to complete a full manual recount may be substantial, particularly in a populous county, and may require several days." (In their December 11, 2000, decision in this case, the court added the obvious observation that "the time required to complete a manual recount must be reasonable. Otherwise, the recount provision would be, in effect, meaningless. Courts should construe statutes to give effect to all provisions, and not to render any part meaningless.")

The manual recount section of the Florida Election Code, then, conflicts with sections 102.111 and 102.112 which state that the canvassing boards *must* submit their returns to the secretary of state "by 5:00 P.M. of the seventh day following an election" (i.e., in this case, November 14). For instance, the court pointed out, if a party filed a pre-certification protest to the election on the sixth day following the election and the sample manual recount indicated that a full countywide recount was necessary, the recount, in most cases, would not be completed by the deadline of the seventh day following the election.

The second ambiguity and conflict was in the deadline statutes themselves. Section 102.111, enacted in 1951, provides that if the returns don't come in by 5:00 P.M. on the seventh day following an election, all late returns "shall" be ignored. But in 1989, the Florida legislature enacted

§102.112 to provide that if the returns don't come in before the seventh day, any later returns "may" be ignored. Hence, §102.111 is mandatory, §102.112 is permissive.

The court said that because of this conflict, it had to "resort to traditional rules of statutory construction in order to determine legislative intent." It went on to point out that it was well settled that where two statutory provisions are in conflict, the specific statute controls the general one. Section 102.111 is titled "Elections Canvassing Commission" and its deadline provision is a tangential inclusion, whereas §102.112 is titled "Deadline for Submission of County Returns" and even spells out the precise penalty ($200 for each late day) for canvassing board members who submit late returns.

Second, it is also well settled, the court pointed out, that when two statutes are in conflict, the more recently enacted statute controls the older one. And third, the court cited the standard, boilerplate, statutory construction principle that related statutory provisions must be read together in order to achieve a consistent and "cohesive whole." With this in mind, the court observed that if, as previously mentioned, a protest to a vote is filed on the sixth day following an election, and a full manual recount is required, the canvassing board of the subject county, through no fault of its own, would be "unable to submit its returns to the Department [of State] by 5:00 P.M. on the seventh day following the election. In such a case, if the mandatory provision in §102.111 were given effect, the votes of the county would be ignored for the simple reason that the board was following the dictates of a different section of the code. The legislature could not have intended to penalize county canvassing boards for following the dictates of the code." Here, because of the hundreds of thousands of votes that had to be hand counted in Broward, Palm Beach, and Miami-Dade counties, if the November 14th "deadline" under §102.111 was mechanically applied, the canvassing board of these three south Florida counties would be unable to conduct the manual recount they were authorized to do under section §102.166. The court went on to say that even the United States Supreme Court recognized that in such a situation the recount statute has to prevail. In an Indiana case before the Supreme Court, the court said that "one procedure necessary to guard against irregularity and error in the tabulation of votes is the availability of a recount. Despite the fact that a certificate of election may be issued to the leading candidate within thirty days after the election, the results are not final if a candidate's option to compel a recount is exercised." *Roudebush v. Hartke*, 405 U.S. 15, 25 (1972)

Accordingly, the court ruled that under standard, statutory construction principles, November 14 (seven days after the election) was not a mandatory date under Florida statutory law, chiseled in stone.

No reasonable person with any legal background could possibly say that the court was trespassing beyond the margins of its authority in ruling the way it did. Indeed, even if the court were wrong in its interpretation of the Florida statutes, the U.S. Supreme Court knew there was no basis for its intervening and reversing the Florida Supreme Court's order. Unless, of course, some "federal question" was involved. The Florida Supreme Court, after clearly predicating its ruling on statutory interpretation grounds, gave Bush, and then the five conservative Justices on the U.S. Supreme Court, an opening (not a valid one in any way whatsoever—as indicated, the U.S. Supreme Court conceded this by implication in its eventual *per curiam* opinion) when, after setting forth the basis for its ruling, it parenthetically added that the right to vote is the preeminent right contained in the Florida *Constitution*, "for without this basic freedom all others would be diminished," and said that, "to the extent that the [Florida] legislature may enact laws regulating the electoral process, those laws are valid only if they impose no unreasonable or unnecessary restraints" on the right to vote. "Because election laws are intended to facilitate the right of suffrage, such laws must be liberally construed in favor of the citizen's right to vote."

The Court added that to allow the secretary of state to summarily disenfranchise innocent voters because of the dilatory work of the members of a canvassing board "misses the constitutional mark," going on to say that "we conclude that consistent with the Florida election scheme, the Secretary may reject a board's amended returns only if the returns are submitted so late that their inclusion will preclude a candidate from contesting the certification [in Florida, the 'contest' stage takes place after the certification by the secretary of state] or preclude Florida's voters from participating fully in the federal electoral process." The Florida Supreme Court concluded its decision by ordering the secretary of state to accept all amended returns received by 5:00 P.M. on Sunday, November 26, 2000,* but that if the Office of the Secretary of State was not open that Sunday, then amended returns were to be accepted until 9:00 A.M. on Monday, November 27, 2000. (In their later, December 11, 2000 decision, the Court pointed out that "the November 26, 2000 date gave the counties no more time to complete the recount than they would have had if the [secretary of state] had not forestalled their efforts.")

Little could the Florida Supreme Court possibly know that while they were doing their job applying the law of their state, there were five Supreme Court Justices above them, led by a right-wing ideologue, Antonin Scalia, who were extremely anxious over the possibility that their candidate, Bush, might

---

*Since thousands of votes still had to be hand counted in Broward, Palm Beach, and Miami-Dade counties, the Court said that the "deadline of November 26, 2000, at 5:00 P.M. was established in order to allow maximum time for contests pursuant to section 102.168."

lose, and, it's a fair inference, were dry-washing their hands
waiting for any possible opportunity or opening at all to intervene and frustrate justice and the right of Americans to choose
their president. (More, later, on the Florida Supreme Court's
benign, passing reference to the Florida Constitution.)

November 22, the day following the Florida Supreme
Court's ruling, was a busy day. The Broward, Palm Beach,
and Miami-Dade county canvassing boards were continuing their manual recount.[1] But a few minutes after noon,
one of them, Miami-Dade, who had changed their mind
about recounting all the votes and initially started recounting only 10,500 undervotes, decided to stop their recount,
saying that it would only be fair to recount *all* the votes in
the county (654,000), but they couldn't do this by the
November 26 deadline. Since just a few hours earlier they
had decided they would try to meet the November 26 deadline, there was immediate speculation as to why they had
suddenly and abruptly changed their minds. Just minutes
before they stopped, a very angry mob of Republican protesters stormed their office building, knocking a few people
down (kicking one of them) along the way, and started
shouting "Let us in. Let us in," while banging on the office
doors and picture window of the board. Shortly after, the
board decided to stop their counting of votes. David Leahy,
the county's supervisor of elections, and a member of the
three-man canvassing board, told reporters from the *New
York Times* and *Boston Globe* that, indeed, the violence of
the protesters had influenced his decision to discontinue
the recount. Later, however, he said that he and his colleagues
were not intimidated into changing their minds about
the recount. It is noteworthy that film footage of the near riot
later revealed that many of the protesters were notroutine

'All numbers refer to Notes begining on p. 155.

Miami citizens, but paid staff members of the Republican
Party who had been involved in the national campaign and
had been flown in to Florida from out of state. As the *New
York Times* reported (November 24, 2000): "When the
ruckus was over, the protesters had what they had wanted,
a unanimous vote by the board to call off the hand counting." How the Republicans could possibly argue thereafter
that this very hostile and physically threatening display
right outside the canvassing board's doors was no different
than a Jesse Jackson protest (where protesters are yelling
out on the street) is hard to see.

That same day, November 22, George Bush petitioned
for a writ of certiorari in the U.S. Supreme Court asking the
Court to review and reverse the decision of the Florida
Supreme Court, saying it was a "lawless exercise of judicial
power by the court . . . designed to thwart the will of the
electorate [the people] as well as the considered judgments
of Florida's executive and legislative branches." November
14, Bush argued, was a mandatory statutory deadline under
Florida law, and no votes could be counted after that date.

Since all the Florida Supreme Court was trying to do was
make sure, under the law, that all valid votes by Floridians be
counted, what possible legal theories did Bush have to prevent something, which at least on its face, appeared so right?
Bush, the candidate of the states-rights party, resorted to *federal*, not *state,* law to try to tell those ol' Confederate
Southerners on the Florida Supreme Court that they were in
the major leagues now, and they simply were out of their
depth. Bush made three contentions under federal law: First,
he said the Florida Supreme Court's ruling violated 3 U. S. C.
§5, an obscure law whose legal ancestry dates originally to
March 4, 1789, with a successor statute on February 3, 1887.
How obscure is it? Listen to this. There are annotated codes
that tell the legal researcher all the cases brought under a particular statute in the past in which appellate courts made rul-

ings. Sometimes the annotations go on for fifty pages, with ten to fifteen cases briefly discussed on each page. 3 U.S.C. §5 has been such a hot item that in over two centuries it and its predecessor statutes were on the books, I couldn't find one single case ever previously brought under it, by anyone. But hey, I guess the mindset of the Bush camp was that if the statute would help in any way to prevent these Florida votes from being counted, as the saying goes, "You go, girl."

3 U.S.C. §5 is a very poorly worded and indistinct statute that reads: "If any state shall have provided, by laws enacted prior to the day fixed for the appointment of the electors [the day of the election] for its final determination of any controversy or contest concerning the appointment of all or any of the electors of such state, by judicial or other methods or procedures, and such determination shall have been made at least six days before the time fixed for the meeting of the electors, such determination made pursuant to such law so existing on said day, and made at least six days prior to said time of meeting of the electors, shall be conclusive, and shall govern in the counting of the electoral votes as provided in the Constitution, and as hereinafter regulated, so far as the ascertainment of the electors appointed by such state is concerned." Whew! Since under federal law (3 U.S.C. §7) the state electors meet and vote on December 18, the determination of who those electors are should be made, per 3 U.S.C. §5, at least six days earlier; that is, December 12.

Bush argued that 3 U.S.C. §5 requires that election "disputes be resolved in accordance with laws enacted prior to election day," and that when the Florida Supreme Court, in resolving the dispute, said that refusing to count all of the counties' returns is such a "drastic measure" that it is appropriate only when they are submitted to the secretary of state so late "that their inclusion will compromise the integrity of the electoral process," the Florida court was enacting a *new* rule of law not in existence "prior to election day" that extended the supposedly mandatory deadline date for counting votes from November 14 to November 26.

But the obvious problem with Bush's contention was that no new law was enacted by the Florida Supreme Court. The court was simply making a *statutory interpretation* of laws (i.e., Sections 102.111, 102.112, and 102.166) already in existence long *before* the election. In thousands upon thousands of cases throughout the years, appellate courts have looked at a statute, or two conflicting statutes, and crafted an interpretation of what they (reasonably or not) believed was the legislative intent behind the statute. (Listen to Chief Justice Rehnquist in his December 12 concurring opinion in this case: "Surely when the Florida legislature empowered the courts of the state to grant 'appropriate' relief, it *must have meant* . . .") That's why it is extremely common for a statute with, let's say, thirty or forty words in it, to be the source of hundreds of appellate court cases in which thousands of pages are written by judges trying to determine what those few words mean. Uppermost in this endeavor is to try to determine (without disinterring from their graves the legislators who enacted the statute) what the legislators who enacted said statute intended. And when there is a conflict between two statutes, the court has to reconcile them in a manner that is consistent with the overall statutory scheme.

For the proposition of determining legislative intent, which is almost too obvious and well-known, really, to state, at least among lawyers, one can cite none other than Justice Scalia, who dispensed with all pretense of impartiality with his December 9, 2000, stay order: "I am not so naive (nor do I think our forebears were) as to be unaware that judges, in a real sense, 'make' law," he wrote in a concurring opinion in *James B. Beam Distilling Company v. Georgia*, 501 U.S. 529, 549 (1991). "But they make it as judges make it, which is to say as though they were 'finding' it—discerning what the law *is*, rather than decreeing what it is today changed *to*."

Moreover, the very title of 3 U.S.C. §5 ("Determination of Controversy as to Appointment of Electors") and its subsequent language strongly indicate, as the Florida attorney general said, that the statute's only intent was to "confer immunity on a properly certified slate of electors from objections lodged in Congress," not to be a mandatory deadline date for the counting of votes and appeals taken thereon.* 3 U.S.C. §5 appears to be a means for addressing situations in which more than one slate of electors claim to represent the same state. Indeed, in the congressional debate on the statute (Act of February 3, 1887, ch.90, s.224 Stat.373), Representative William Craig Cooper of Ohio said, "These contests, these disputes between *rival* electors, between persons claiming to have been appointed electors, should be settled under a law made prior to the day when such contests are to be decided." (18 Congressional Record 47, December 8, 1886)

3 U.S.C.§5 has merely been referred to by legal scholars as a "safe harbor" statute, not a deadline for the counting of votes. As Lis Wiehl, constitutional law professor at the University of Washington in Seattle, told me: "If a state is truly interested in appointing electors who represent the majority vote of the people of the state, wouldn't they rather forego the certainty of the safe harbor and continue the vote so as to get the right result? Isn't it better to get the

---

*Perhaps the best evidence that 3 U.S.C. § 5 is not considered to be a deadline for counting votes is that Bush *himself*, in his last appeal to the U.S. Supreme Court on December 10, only maintained that 3 U.S.C. § 5 "creates a 'safe harbor' for a state insofar as congressional consideration of its electoral votes is concerned." His brief goes on to say that 3 U.S.C. § 5 prohibits the enactment of laws to resolve election disputes that were not in existence prior to the election on November 7, and alleges that the Florida Supreme Court enacted said laws. But nowhere did the Bush brief expressly allege that December 12 was a mandatory deadline date for the counting of votes.

result that the voters intended? And just because the vote does not get certified under the ambit of the safe harbor provision doesn't mean that Congress would challenge electors certified after the safe harbor date of December 12. What reason could Congress possibly have for doing this?" Indeed, in 1960, Congress accepted a slate of electors from Hawaii that wasn't appointed until January 4, 1961, three weeks after the December 12 "deadline."

Of course, we know that here the Florida legislature, overwhelmingly Republican and pro-Bush, was making threats to appoint their own Republican slate of electors even if the vote in Florida ended up going for Gore. But if they did that, it would be such a tyrannical, fascist act, and so antithetical to everything this nation stands for, that *even* the media might treat it as worse than Clinton trying to cover up a private, consensual affair. (But I can't be sure of this.) And also, of course, this may have only been saber-rattling by the Republican legislators. After all, they are all politicians who would have to worry about coming up for reelection.[2]

Bush next argued that the Florida Supreme Court's decision also violated Art.2, §1, cl.2 of the U.S. Constitution, which provides: "Each state shall appoint, in such manner as the legislature thereof may direct, a number of electors, equal to the whole number of senators and representatives to which the state may be entitled in the Congress . . ." How did the Florida Supreme Court decision violate Article 2? According to Bush, "any decision overriding the Florida legislature's procedures for appointing electors (including the November 14 deadline for certifying votes) would violate Article 2, which vests sole authority over such matters in the legislatures of the several states." In effect, Bush was arguing that Article 2's delegation to state legislatures of the authority to determine the manner in which presidential electors are appointed eliminated the state courts' power to

interpret state law. But obviously, although the state legislatures enact laws to appoint electors, like all state laws, the
meaning of these state laws has to be determined by state
courts.

Although it was clear that Bush, in his legal architecture,
was stretching in every direction to find some authority, anywhere, *to prevent* all the votes from being counted in
Florida, in his November 22, 2000, petition for certiorari he
had the unbelievable, monumental gall to argue that "the
American public's right to vote is one of the most sacred protected by our Constitution. . . . The Florida Supreme Court's
decision poses a clear and present danger to that right." In
other words, it was that rotten, swinish Al Gore and Florida
Supreme Court who were trying to deprive people of their
right to vote. Black is white and white is black in the world of
politics and lawyers who turn their mother's picture against
the wall and say anything at all to win. There's no shame, no
embarrassment. For anything.

I may be wrong, but I believe it should be obvious to any
fair and objective person that only someone searching for a
legal technicality to get around what is right and decent and
honorable would ever resort, in these circumstances, to
arguments like Article 2 and Title 3.

Bush's third and last federal argument was that the lack of
a uniform standard in the various Florida counties to count
votes violated the equal protection clause of the Fourteenth
Amendment to the United States Constitution. On
November 24, the U.S. Supreme Court granted Bush's writ of
certiorari (i.e., agreed to review the decision of the Florida
Supreme Court) "on questions one and two [Article 2 and
Title 3 grounds, but not equal protection] as presented by the
petition."

As indicated earlier, on November 21, 2000, the Florida
Supreme Court had extended the recount deadline to
Sunday, November 26, at 5:00 P.M. (And on November 22,

the Miami-Dade County canvassing board voted not to proceed with a manual recount. On November 23, the Florida Supreme Court unanimously refused an emergency petition by Gore to compel the Miami-Dade canvassing board to resume its manual recount.) The manual recount *was* completed in Broward county by the new November 26 deadline, with Gore picking up 567 net votes, but the Palm Beach canvassing board, after taking Thanksgiving off, did not complete its recount by the Sunday deadline.

On the afternoon of November 26, feeling that his canvassing board would not be able to meet the 5:00 P.M. deadline, Judge Burton, the canvassing board's chairman, rushed off a faxed letter to Secretary of State Katherine Harris pleading for a little more time. "We have been working diligently, including the last 24 hour period," he wrote, "to complete this critical portion of the hand count. Your consideration of our request to extend the deadline for final submission of this hand count until Monday, November 27, at 9:00 A.M. [which the Florida Supreme Court, it should be recalled, authorized Harris to do] would be greatly appreciated, as we know you are interested in counting all votes . . ." Harris promptly faxed back a reply denying the request. Burton told the press that in view of what was at stake and the twenty hour days that his vote counters had been putting in, "a couple of hours should not make any difference."

At 4:54 that afternoon, Burton faxed in to Harris certified amended returns from 584 out of Palm Beach County's 637 precincts (with 174 net votes for Gore), but Harris refused to accept them, saying she would only accept all of the returns or none.

(The following, though a partial tributary from what preceded it, is offered only because it is reflective of the vulgar banality of politics and the hypocrisy of conservative Republicans who, far more than their counterparts on the

left, want everyone to know about how much they love
America and all of the values and principles it represents.)
Harris is the multimillionaire granddaughter of a Florida
citrus and cattle baron who should have recused herself in
this election (as Bush's brother, Jeb, the governor of
Florida, had the decency to do) since she not only campaigned for Bush in the snow of New Hampshire and was
a delegate to the Republican National Convention in
Philadelphia, but, more important, was a cochairwoman of
Bush's campaign in Florida. Everything about Harris, from
her garish layers of makeup, abundant jewelry, and her utter-
ances ("I feel so historic," she purred giddily at the height of
the controversy), to her spending more money on traveling
during her first two years as secretary of state (a largely cere-
monial position in Florida that will be eliminated in 2002)
than any other public official, including the governor,
bespeaks of her being a lightweight. Indeed, when the U.S.
Commission on Civil Rights conducted two days of hearings
in Tallahassee in January investigating all the serious problems in Florida's presidential election, she irritated and frus-
trated commission members no end by repeatedly referring
questions to her assistant. "I stand accountable," she told the
commission, "but I will still have to refer to Mr. [Clay]
Roberts. He does the day-to-day operations." The chair-
woman of the commission, Mary Frances Berry, called
Harris's testimony "laughable. I feel it's a sad commentary.
She neither saw nor seems interested in the kinds of problems we have been seeing here." But though Harris was a
lightweight, she just happened to be in a position from which
she could effortlessly deliver a heavyweight, knockout blow.

Knowing what we do about Harris, although I am not a
gambling man I would wager she had never been to her
office on a Sunday before (Judge Charles Burton told me
"You definitely would not have found Harris in her office on
a Sunday, I guarantee you that"), and even though the Florida

Supreme Court told her that if she didn't open up the office
on the Sunday in question, there would be no problem
accepting returns up to 9:00 A.M. on Monday, this perfectly
wonderful woman, who is a state officer representing *all* the
citizens of the state, not just Republicans, hopped in her car
that Sunday and went down, lickety-split, to open her office.
She may not have known how to run her office in an election, but she certainly knew what side she was on in the election, and anything she could do to get her candidate elected,
you could count her in, even if it meant not counting valid
votes of fellow Floridians. This, of course, is what Harris
would have wanted a secretary of state who was a Democrat
to do if the shoe were on the other foot—open up the office
on a Sunday to make sure that valid votes that reached her
office before nine the next morning would not be counted.
Calling Harris's conduct disgusting is too mild.

As it turned out, the Palm Beach County Board did get *all*
of its votes in about two hours after the 5:00 P.M. deadline, at
7:07 P.M., with 215 net votes for Gore. Since Harris hadn't
yet certified the Florida election for Bush, she could easily
have accepted them, but naturally, Harris did not. Later, at
7:30 P.M., Harris, undoubtedly with a swelling sense of pride
and happiness within, certified Florida's twenty-five electoral
votes for her guy, Bush. The vote was 2,912,719 for Bush,
and 2,912, 253 for Gore, a difference of 537 votes.

A postcript about Harris. The nasty lassie from Tallahassee
is the same person who once told a reporter that she didn't
like "gamesmanship" in politics. The same person who
admits to dreaming of being appointed an ambassador in the
Bush administration, saying she is "passionately interested"
in it. The same person who recruited General Norman
Schwarzkopf, known widely in Florida and elsewhere to be a
Bush supporter, to do a taxpayer-funded get-out-the-vote ad
for her office during the Florida campaign. One of Harris's
closest advisers during the election controversy was a very

influential Tallahassee lawyer-lobbyist named J.M. Stipanovich who was known to have unusually close ties to Jeb Bush. As reported in *Newsweek* (November 25), "After last year's session of the state legislature, Stipanovich, who represents Big Sugar, among other interests, was overheard telling Jeb Bush, 'I got everything. I don't know what the poor people got, but the rich people are happy and I'm ready to go home.' This, again, was one of the key people who had Harris's ear during the election controversy. A friend of Harris from her hometown of Sarasota, Florida, told reporters during Harris' performance in the controversy: "This is a heavily Republican area. No matter what happens, I'll bet the next time Katherine comes to Sarasota for an opera opening, she'll get a standing ovation when she walks in." If I were there, I'd stand, too. I've always taken my hat off to outrageous individuals. After all, it's not easy to become who they are.

November 27, the day after Harris certified Florida's twenty-five electoral votes for Bush, Gore filed a complaint in Leon County contesting the certification of the election. The entire process that led up to the November 26 certification was under §102.166 of the Florida Election Code ("Protest of Election Returns"). Section 102.168 ("Contest of Election") comes into play only *after* the certification of the election and sets forth grounds for setting aside the result of the election, one of which, under §102.168(3)(c), is the "rejection of a number of legal votes sufficient to change or place in doubt the election." Here, Gore alleged that the following legal (i.e., valid) votes were improperly rejected by Harris: (1) 215 net votes for Gore identified in a manual recount by the Palm Beach canvassing board which, the board concluded, reflected the clear intent of the voter. Section 101.5614 of the Florida Election Code provides that "no vote shall be declared invalid or void if there is a clear indication of the intent of the voter as determined by the canvassing board." Section 102.166(7)(b) also provides that "if a counting team is unable to determine a voter's intent in casting a ballot, the ballot shall be presented to the County canvassing board for it to determine the voter's intent." (2) 168 net votes for Gore identified in the partial recount (before the board stopped their count on November 22, 2000) by the Miami-Dade County canvassing board.

Gore also asked that approximately 9,000 undervotes that were left uncounted when the Miami-Dade canvassing board stopped their recount on November 22 now be manually recounted.

The case came before Judge N. Sanders Sauls of the Leon County Circuit Court in Tallahassee for trial (actually, an evidentiary hearing). Since time was of the essence, in that December 12 was being erroneously considered as a deadline for the counting of all votes and appeals based thereon, on November 28 Gore's lawyers pleaded with Sauls to accelerate the start of the trial, but Sauls refused, setting the trial date for December 2, meaning the Gore camp lost several precious days.* And once the trial started, Sauls,

---

*While the Gore team was waiting to start the trial in Judge Sauls' courtroom, on December 1, the Florida Supreme Court dealt the Gore camp a setback when it refused to order a revote in Palm Beach County requested in a lawsuit brought by several Palm Beach County residents "and others similarly situated" on the ground that the butterfly ballot used in the county was not only confusing to many voters, but more importantly, was illegal. Contrary to some reports at the time that Florida law required that voting squares be to the right of a candidate's name, it does not. §101.5609 (6) does say, however, that "voting squares may be placed in front of [i.e., to the right of] or in back of [to the left of] the names of candidates," the implication, I would think, being that a ballot may use one or the other design, but not both. (In the butterfly ballot, the square for Pat Buchanan was to the *left* of his name and sandwiched *between* squares to the *right* of Bush's and Gore's names.) Also, §101.191 sets forth a form for a general election, saying that ballots "shall be substantially" in the form that followed, which had squares to the *right* of the names of all candidates for President and Vice-President. However, the Florida Supreme Court ruled that "even accepting appellants' allegations, we conclude as a matter of law that the Palm Beach County ballot does not constitute substantial non-compliance with the statutory requirements" which would justify a revote in the county.

who showed a distinct preference in his tone and demeanor to the Bush team of lawyers, insisted on moving at his own elephantine pace, allowing, for example, very lengthy direct and cross-examinations, and showing up twenty minutes late in his own courtroom, all to the unconcealed pleasure of the Bush team.

Both sides (Bush and Gore) called witnesses[3] and gave oral arguments to Sauls, a former prosecutor and lobbyist with a Southern drawl and country ways who has a reputation for being a man of few words. During the December 2–4, 2000, trial, the rest of the world outside of Tallahassee found out why the laconic Sauls was so stingy with his words. Sauls says very little because he apparently is smart enough to know he has nothing to say. When he did talk at the trial, he showed he had no more business presiding over this historic case than the local cabby, making one gross legal blunder after another.

After Sauls ruled in favor of Bush on December 4, saying that none of Gore's contentions had merit, Gore immediately appealed to Florida's First District Court of Appeal, which certified the case, without reviewing it, up to the Florida Supreme Court. The court reversed Saul's ruling on December 8, saying he had made the following indisputable legal errors:

1. Saul's December 4 ruling said that with respect to the decision of the Miami-Dade canvassing board not to continue the recount, "local [canvassing] boards have been given broad discretion which no court may overrule, absent a clear abuse of discretion." Sauls said he found no such abuse of discretion. But the Florida Supreme Court noted that "the *trial* court in a *contest* action in Florida does not sit as an *appellate* court over the decisions of the canvassing board. . . . A contest proceeding . . . is filed in the circuit [trial] court and addresses the validity of the election itself . . . Accordingly, while the board's actions concerning the

election process may constitute evidence in a contest proceeding, the board's decisions are not to be accorded the highly deferential 'abuse of discretion' standard of review. . . . In the present case, the trial court erroneously applied an appellate abuse of discretion standard" to the decision of the Miami-Dade canvassing board.

2. Unbelievably, Sauls did not even know the burden of proof that had to be satisfied by Gore in order to prevail. That's like a judge in a criminal case not knowing that the prosecution has the burden of proving guilt "beyond a reasonable doubt," or the judge in a civil action not knowing that the plaintiff has to prove his case "by a preponderance of the evidence." Sauls, in his ruling, said that "it is well established . . . that in order to contest election results under §102.168 of the Florida statutes, the plaintiff must show that, but for the irregularity or inaccuracy claimed, the result of the election would have been different, and he or she would have been the winner." Sauls cited an old 1982 Florida appeals court case that held that "it is not enough to show a reasonable possibility that election results could have been altered by such irregularities; rather, a reasonable probability that the results of the election would have been changed must be shown." Sauls said Gore hadn't met his very high burden of proof.

What the painfully incompetent Sauls apparently did not know was that he was articulating the old law of Florida, that the Florida legislature had since changed the burden of proof by lowering it considerably. Section 102.168(3)(c), enacted by the Florida legislature in 1999, clearly reads that the contesting candidate merely has to show that there was a "rejection of a number of legal votes sufficient to change *or place in doubt* the result of the election." It is nothing short of incredible that Sauls, presiding over this extremely important trial, would not even know the current law applicable to the case. Although Sauls had referred to §102.168 in his order, he apparently had never even opened up the book and actually looked at it. Unbelievable.[4]

3. Over one million ballots from Palm Beach and Miami-Dade counties (only 14,000 of which were undervotes that Gore was contesting) had been trucked up to the Leon County courthouse in Tallahassee, and Gore's chief trial lawyer, David Boies, urged Sauls, as the trier of fact, to examine at least some of the undervotes as evidence to prove there were, indeed, many valid votes among them that clearly showed the intent of the voter. For instance, a situation where the voter had punched, with his stylus, a hole in the paper ballot for a particular candidate to the point where one could see light, yet the chad was still attached (hanging) by one or more of its four sides. In that situation, the Votomatic machine many times does not detect the vote, though under §101.5614(5) of the Florida Elections Code his intent could not be any clearer. Such legal and valid undervotes were the "best evidence" that Gore had to support his contention that many valid votes had not been counted, thus justifying a manual recount of the remaining 9,000 Miami-Dade undervotes. Although it would be the equivalent of a trial judge or a jury refusing to look at the evidence proffered by a party to the lawsuit, the remarkable Sauls did just that, absolutely refusing to look at even one undervote. Sauls thereby enunciated a new rule of law for the ages, which in deference to him I want to italicize. *The very best way to determine whether evidence is valid or invalid is to not look at it.* As the Florida Supreme Court said about Sauls, "Without ever examining or investigating the ballots that the machines failed to register as a vote, the trial court in this case concluded that there was no probability of a different result . . . By failing to examine the specifically identified group of uncounted ballots that is claimed to contain the rejected legal votes, the trial court has refused to address the [very] issue presented."

In reversing Sauls on December 8, the Florida Supreme

Court ordered the Miami-Dade canvassing board to immediately commence manually recounting the remaining
9,000 undervotes.* The court said that "*through no fault of
appellant* (Gore), a lawfully commenced manual recount in
Dade County was never completed, and recounts that were
completed were not counted . . . There can be no question
that there are legal votes within the 9,000 uncounted votes
sufficient to place the results of this election *in doubt*. We
know this not only by evidence of statistical analysis but also
by the actual experience of recounts conducted. The votes
for each candidate that have been counted are separated by
no more than approximately 500 votes and may be separated
by as little as approximately 100 votes. Thousands of
uncounted votes could obviously make a difference . . . *We
must do everything required by law to ensure that legal votes
that have not been counted are included in the final election
results.*"

The court, in a footnote, observed that the three dissenting justices on the seven man court "would have us throw up
our hands and say that because of looming deadlines and
practical difficulties we should give up any attempt to have
the election of the presidential electors rest upon the vote of
Florida citizens as mandated by the legislature. While we
agree that practical difficulties may well end up controlling

---

*You will recall that on November 23, the Florida Supreme Court had refused
to compel the Miami-Dade canvassing board to resume the manual recount they
stopped after the near-riot outside its doors by Republican protestors. By its now
ordering the same board to do the very thing it had refused to order earlier, was
the Florida Supreme Court being contradictory? No. The previous rejection was
during the "protest" stage of the election where, under Florida law [Sections
102.166 (4) and (5)] the canvassing boards are the ones who have the discretion
to bring about relief to the protesting candidate. But the court's ruling on
December 8 was during the "contest" stage, where Florida law gives the courts,
not the canvassing boards, the broad authority under Section 102.168(8) to "provide any relief appropriate under the circumstances."

the outcome of the election, we vigorously disagree that we should therefore abandon our responsibility to resolve this election dispute under the rule of law. We can only do the best we can to carry out our sworn responsibilities to the justice system and its role in this process."

The court also ordered that the 215 net votes for Gore in Palm Beach County and the 168 net votes for Gore in Miami-Dade be included in the certified results of the election. *Bush's lead had shrunk to but 154 votes.* (As indicated earlier, after the second machine recount on November 9, Bush's original lead of 1,784 votes had been shaved to 327. Since Gore thereafter picked up a total of 848 net votes from the hand counts (98 in Volusia, 567 in Broward, 215 in Palm Beach and 168 in Miami-Dade), why was Bush still ahead by 154 votes? He received well over 600 more net absentee overseas ballots than Gore.)

Finally, the court ordered that each of the sixty-seven counties in the entire state, not just the original four counties, commence manually counting all undervotes in their respective counties "forthwith." (Bush, of course, immediately filed both an appeal to the U.S. Supreme Court of the Florida court's ruling and a petition to the high court to stay (stop) the Florida recount.) The counting throughout Florida commenced the next morning, December 9, at 8:00 A.M. It was obvious to everybody that Al Gore might very well become our next president.

Less than one thousand miles to the north, five conservative Supreme Court Justices, led by the judicial darling of the right wing, Antonin Scalia, were having kittens over the new developments in the case below. Before any possible story came out of Florida that Gore had overcome Bush in Florida (which would change the entire complexion and dynamics of the election, making Gore the front-runner in the eyes of the nation and thus making it much more unlikely that the court's dirty work in doing whatever they could for their candidate, Bush, would be acceptable to the American people), Scalia stepped in at 2:00 P.M. that same day to halt the Florida vote. Of the five Justices, only Scalia signed the stay order.

I now take the reader back to the *Nation* article for the Supreme Court's subsequent decision three days later handing the election to Bush. But before I do, I want to mention two important points.

Most Republicans throughout the nation have had a quick response to the claim by Democrats that the U.S. Supreme Court, seven out of nine of whose members are Republican, stole the election for Bush. What about the Florida Supreme Court?they say. They (six out of seven are Democrats) were trying to steal it for Gore. But in the first place, unlike the U.S. Supreme Court, there is no evidence that the Florida Supreme Court based its decisions on anything but solid and enduring legal principles. Therefore, there was no indication that they were attempting to help Gore at Bush's expense. But even if we were to assume, just for the sake of argument, that the Florida Supreme Court was out to help Gore and they did so by deliberately bending and distorting the law the way we know the U.S. Supreme Court did to help Bush, there would still be an enormous difference between the two courts, so enormous that even if, as I say, we assume the worst of the Florida court, its conduct should not even be discussed in the same breath with that of the U.S. Supreme Court. I say that because there's absolutely nothing that the Florida court did that is reflective of criminal intent. *You don't steal an election by wanting all valid votes to be counted.* The Florida Supreme Court wanted all valid votes to be counted. The U.S. Supreme Court wanted valid votes *not* to be counted. When you separate the wheat from the chaff and look at the inherent morality, or lack thereof, of the two courts, there is no comparison.

Second, I say several places in the *Nation* article that the U.S. Supreme Court was looking for a way, any way at all, to steal the election for their candidate, Bush. This somewhat implies that they also looked into theories other than the bogus equal protection one to save the day for Bush. Although the evidence is not conclusive, it is very persuasive that this, indeed, is what happened. I mentioned earlier that Bush, in his legal arguments, maintained that the Florida Supreme Court, in its November 21 ruling extending the vote-counting deadline from November 14 to November 26, not only violated 3U.S.C.§5 but violated Article 2, §1, cl.2 of the U.S. Constitution because it overrode the Florida legislature's procedures for appointing electors, something that, under Article 2 he argued it could not do since Article 2 vests sole authority over such matters with the legislature. But the Florida legislature, after being delegated the power under Article 2 of the U.S. Constitution to decide the "manner" in which electors are appointed, enacted statutes in Florida to carry out that responsibility. The bottom line to Bush's argument, were it accepted, is that the Florida Supreme Court was powerless and had no right to interpret these Florida statutes (enacted by the Florida legislature) dealing with the election. Not only would this be nonsensical even if the Florida legislature had not spoken on the issue (since there have been a great number of court cases in Florida where the courts have interpreted and ruled upon the Florida election statutes), but it did. Section 102.168 (1), the Florida "contest" statute enacted by Bush's beloved Florida legislature, provides that unsuccessful candidates may contest the election "in the circuit court." Unless Bush thought that the legislature only intended the circuit court to lend a sympathetic ear, with coffee and doughnuts, to the unsuccessful candidate, there's no question that the legislature intended the court system of Florida, with judicial review to Florida's

Supreme Court, to handle litigation arising out of Florida elections.

The belief by many is that early on the U.S. Supreme Court started focusing in more on another argument by Bush that Bush hadn't emphasized nearly as much. It was a more subtle, intellectually palatable spin, they may have thought, on Article 2. Yes, the Florida Supreme Court clearly had the power and the right to interpret Florida election law. But as indicated earlier, in its November 21 ruling, after spending the majority of its opinion on its rigorous interpretation of Florida *statutory* law, the Florida Supreme Court added that it also found support for its opinion in the Florida *Constitution*. Ah hah, the five Justices apparently felt. This might be the opening we need. If the Florida Supreme Court based its decision on the Florida Constitution, we can argue that Article 2 of the U.S. Constitution grants state legislatures the exclusive power to enact statutes concerning the appointment of presidential electors *outside* the reach of *state constitutional* limitations. But since it wasn't clear to the U.S. Supreme Court whether the Florida Supreme Court based its November 21 decision on an interpretation of Florida *statutory* law (which would be permissible) or Florida *constitutional* law (which, at least according to the Justices, would not), on December 4, pursuant to the writ of certiorari it had granted Bush on November 24 for his Article 2 and Title 3 arguments (but not equal protection), the court said: "We are unclear as to the extent to which the Florida Supreme Court saw the Florida *Constitution* as circumscribing the [Florida] legislature's authority under Article 2, §1, cl.2. We are also unclear as to the consideration the Florida Supreme Court accorded to 3 U.S.C.§5. The judgment of the Supreme Court of Florida [the November 21 ruling of the Florida Supreme Court extending the vote-counting deadline to November 26] is therefore vacated and the case is remanded for further proceedings not inconsistent with this opinion."

The cryptic December 4 U.S. Supreme Court ruling was widely perceived by the legal community as being more pro-Bush than pro-Gore. After all, the court *had* vacated the Florida Supreme Court's decision. The further belief was that the court was seeking, without expressly asking for, a clarification from the lower court as to the basis for its ruling extending the vote-counting deadline, and that the conservative wing of the U.S. Supreme Court was spoiling to prevent all further recounts on the grounds that such a recount would somehow, in a legally arcane way, violate Article 2, §1 cl.2 of the U.S. Constitution, as well as Title 3, §5, the supposed "new law" prohibition. Indeed, if the Florida Supreme Court had crafted a "new law" in apparent violation of Title 3, that would trigger a violation of Article 2, since only the Florida legislature could enact new election laws.

But in an ostensible snub of the court upstairs, the Florida Supreme Court did not immediately respond with a clarifying decision for the higher court, probably out of irritation, probably because they knew the Article 2, Title 3 arguments were baseless and fraudulent, and also knew that their November 21 decision made it clear to anyone (other than those with Machiavellian designs, such as the U.S. Supreme Court) that they based their ruling on a plain, simple, traditional interpretation of Florida's statutory law. Days went by, and still no word from the Florida Supreme Court, which was no longer concerning itself with its November 21 ruling (set aside by the U.S. Supreme Court) arising out of Florida's "protest" laws, since on December 8 it had now ordered a recount under Florida's "contest" laws.

The silence from the lower court probably pleased the

five conservative justices. It would just make it easier to set aside the recount under Article 2 and Title 3.

But on the evening of December 11, 2000, the night before the U.S. Supreme Court's ruling handing the election to Bush, the Florida Supreme Court finally issued an opinion responding to the U.S. Supreme Court in which they appeared to completely cut the legs out from under the felonious five. The Florida court set forth, once again, all their legal rationale for their November 21 ruling, but then, in clear and unambiguous language, said that it had "been faced with a question of the statutory construction of Florida's election laws in accord with the intent of the Florida legislature. Our examination of that issue has been *limited* to a determination of legislative intent as informed by the traditional sources and rules of construction we have long accepted as relevant in determining such intent." The court went on to declare that "no new rules of state law" had been formulated by them. They had simply interpreted Florida laws "enacted long before the present election took place." Inasmuch as the U.S. Supreme Court itself, in its December 4 ruling, said that "as a general rule, this court defers to a state court's interpretation of a state statute," the felonious five were put in a desperate situation by the lower court's decision. There was no "federal question" for them to base any pro-Bush ruling on.

Now let's go to a front-page story by Joan Biskupic in the January 22, 2001, edition of *USA Today* that has a ring of truth to it because it is perfectly harmonious with everything else that we know about this case. Biskupic, who covers the high court for *USA Today*, writes that her report was based on "an examination of the court's activities and *interviews with more than two dozen people close to the justices*." She writes: "On December 12, a flurry of holiday cheer in the [Supreme Court] building masked the wrenching negotiations behind the scenes over the Florida case. As a team of workers put colored lights on the court's 22-foot Christmas tree in the Great Hall, the nine justices were in their chambers wrangling over the law. At the start, it didn't seem so hard. In the early deliberations, the five conservative justices who on December 9 had halted the recounts ordered by the Florida Supreme Court—O'Connor, Rehnquist, Scalia, Thomas, and Anthony Kennedy— seemed to be on the same page. In fact, Rehnquist initially believed a decision would come December 11, the day the court heard oral arguments in the historic case. The chief kept the courthouse staff on duty late that day [December 11]. But shortly after the staff ordered Chinese carry-out, it was told to go home. One factor that complicated things was a decision by the Florida Supreme Court *that evening* in which the state court clarified its grounds for intervening in the ballot controversy. That made it more difficult for the Justices to assert that the state panel had improperly set new rules of state law." Biskupic goes on to say that the five justices then "fractured into two camps: Rehnquist, Scalia and Thomas, who continued to say that the Florida court had acted illegally and infringed on legislative power; and O'Connor and Kennedy, who agreed any recounts would be improper but for a different reason—the different standards that Florida counties had been using for recounts. They believed this could violate the Constitution's guarantee of equal protection under the law. . . . What finally was released the night of December 12, two hours before a midnight deadline that would have raised the possibility of congressional intervention, was a thin mix of precedent and legal reasoning. The court's decision stopping the recounts was a novel interpretation of the Constitution's guarantee of equal protection that included a declaration that the ruling shouldn't affect other cases."

If the reader will allow me to be a fly on the wall in some room of the marble and mahogany splendor of the U.S.

Supreme Court Building in Washington, D.C. on the
evening of December 11 following receipt of the Florida
high court's ruling, I can imagine hearing a conversation
among the five high-heeled ladies of the night, the essence
of which went something like this: Scalia: "Now what in the
hell do we do? Those SOBs down there in Tallahassee just
couldn't leave well enough alone, could they? I say we go
ahead with Article 2, Title 3 anyway. We're the U.S.
Supreme Court, damn it. If we can't do whatever we want,
who in the hell can?" Rehnquist and Thomas: "We're
aboard." O'Connor to Scalia, Thomas and Rehnquist: "After
what the Tallahassee court said, how can we proceed on
Article 2, Title 3 grounds? We'll be crucified by the media."
Scalia: "Media, shmedia. The media don't know their der-
riere from a hole in the ground." Kennedy: "I don't know. I
just don't feel comfortable with Article 2, Title 3 anymore.
But hey, like you three, Sandra and I are more than willing
to be a part of this judicial heist, but gee, at least for our
progeny's sake, don't force us to put our names to an opinion that talks about Article 2, §1, cl.2, and 3 U.S.C. §5,
which not one out of ten thousand Americans has ever
heard of. At least an equal protection violation might *sound*
good to most people." O'Connor: "Right. It'll make us sound
like we care—you know, everybody should be treated equally." Rehnquist: "The only problem, for Chrissake, is that just
three weeks ago we said the equal protection argument was
so bad we wouldn't even consider it. What about *our* progeny?" O'Connor and Kennedy: "Well, you've raised a good
point." Rehnquist to O'Connor and Kennedy: "Look, I run
this crime family, so I'm going to make the decision here. We
all agree that I have to swear in Junior on the twentieth of
next month. All we can do on this decision is cut our losses.
We'll go equal protection, but only if you two write the opinion, since it's your bright idea." O'Connor and Kennedy:
"Thanks, Chief. We'll owe you one."

As I pointed out at the beginning of this *Summary*, after all the legal wrangling you have just read about, the United States Supreme Court, in its *per curiam* majority ruling on December 12, 2000, found no legal errors or impropriety on the part of the Florida Supreme Court; that is, with the sole exception of its stating that the Florida court, "with the power to assure uniformity has ordered a statewide recount with minimal procedural safeguards." The legal as well as moral bankruptcy of those words are discussed elsewhere in this book. But it must be reiterated at this point that the standard the Florida Supreme Court established for the counting of the undervotes, that a vote should be considered valid "if there is a clear intent of the voter," comes straight out of Florida statutory law. (§101.5614(5) of the Florida Election Code) So the U.S. Supreme Court, in effect, ruled that the Florida Supreme Court violated the Equal Protection Clause of the Fourteenth Amendment by following the law enacted by the Florida legislature.

But knowing, as we do, that the five justices were only interested in finding some way, any way at all, to give the election to Bush, if the Florida Supreme Court *had* departed from Florida statutory law and established a different and more specific uniform standard, as sure as God made green apples the U.S. Supreme Court would have pounced on this like a hungry tiger going after raw meat. The lower court, the Supremes would have said, had enacted "new" law not in existence "prior to the election" in violation of 3 U.S.C. §5, and the Supreme Court would have likewise prevented any counting of the undervotes.

In other words, the Florida Supreme Court was in a Catch-22 situation. One can't win when the other side not only holds all the cards, but has the morals of an alley cat.

SUMMARY OF LEGAL PROCEEDINGS (BUSH v. GORE)

NOTE ONE

THE CONSTANT CHARGE by Republicans during the election controversy was that the hand recount was completely unreliable because biased Democratic vote counters were running amok "seeing" votes for Gore that were not actually discernible, and hence, did not exist. Really? Is that why, in the manual recounts in Broward, Palm Beach, and Volusia counties, and the aborted recount in Miami-Dade, the net votes picked up by Gore were not enough to overcome Bush's razor-thin lead? When I asked Judge Charles E. Burton, chairman of the Palm Beach canvassing board, about the charges, he labeled them "ridiculous." Burton said the procedures set up in Palm Beach County were "representative" of the other three counties. In Palm Beach county, there were thirty teams of vote counters, each team having one Democrat and one Republican. Even though Florida law did not require it, there was a Republican and Democratic observer with each of the thirty teams watching the counting of every vote. (He said that by law, he, a county judge, the county supervisor of elections [Theresa LePore], and a county commissioner [Carol Roberts] had to rule on all "contested, questionable" ballots.) In addition, a group of lawyers from each party was continuously present. As if that wasn't enough, a camera was always on (Channel 20, a Palm Beach County Government and Education channel), televising everything, and one representative each from the print, radio, and TV media were in the room at all times observing the proceedings. "Everything was open and public," Burton said. When I asked him "if a Houdini could have pulled off a fast one" under the exceedingly heavy scrutiny existing in the counting room, his quick reply was "No."

NOTE TWO

THIS GIVES RISE to a discussion about perhaps the most preposterous, outlandish argument of all by conservative Republicans in the election debate. They argue that the Supreme Court had to do what it did to "avoid a constitutional crisis."* There's only one, not two or more, translations to this assertion by these people. Namely, if an election isn't close, there's no such need for the Supreme Court to intervene. But if an American election is bitterly close, as all close elections are, then it's better for the Supreme Court to pick the president, *whether or not he won the election*, than to have the dispute resolved in the manner prescribed by law. Even if one *wanted* to accept such mindless bilge, how could one do it without first tying up and gagging one's intellect first? Mind you, the barons of buffoonery, sultans of silliness, dukes of duncery who make this argument are not on leashes, but are gainfully employed and leading regular lives. The argument is so insane that to

---

*Indeed, several bootlicking Democrats like Senator Robert Torricelli of New Jersey, who are always seeking to gain the approval of the far right by convincing them they are "good" Democrats (these thickpated simpletons never seem to learn that there is only one way to satisfy these fanatics on the right, and that's to change their registration to Republican), have joined with conservative Republicans in mouthing this exquisite inanity. The silly Torricelli told *Newsweek* magazine (December 25) that we should have "gratitude that the nation dodged a bullet."

rebut it necessarily gives it a dignity it does not have. But since one hears it ad nauseam, and it has been parroted by many in the media, one has little choice but to mention it.

In the first place, when any contest is disputed, in a civilized society you resolve the dispute by turning to the group that has been established for this purpose. What entity in America is supposed to decide what set of presidential electors should be accepted? (Here, if Gore had won the recount, yet the Florida legislature had previously or subsequently chosen 25 electors for Bush, the contest would have been between those electors and 25 electors pledged to vote for Gore.) The Twelfth Amendment to the United States Constitution, ratified in 1804, expressly and explicitly delegates to this nation's Congress the responsibility of counting the electoral votes in all presidential elections, close or not close. Since it's a national election, the choice of Congress to count the votes seems obvious. Necessarily implicit in this delegation of authority to Congress is that Congress has to decide *which* electoral votes shall be counted. And 3 U.S.C. §15, enacted by Congress, expressly says this and details the process.* (The Twelfth

---

*Section 3 U.S.C. §15 provides that where there are rival electors, Congress has to decide which one "is supported by the decision of such state so authorized by *its* law." The Bush electors would argue that under Art. 2, §1, cl.2 of the U.S. Constitution, "each state shall appoint, in such manner as the legislature [in this case the Florida legislature] thereof may direct, a number of electors . . ." and the Florida legislature chose them. But if Gore had won the recount ordered by the Florida Supreme Court, Gore's electors could have argued that Article 2 doesn't say that the state legislature can appoint electors indiscriminately and with absolute discretion. It has to be done "in such manner as the legislature" may direct. What is that "manner" here? The Florida legislature enacted §102.168 of the Florida Election Code, the "contest" statute which was in existence *prior* to the election, thus satisfying any objection under 3 U.S.C. §5. And under this statute, the Florida legislature gave the Florida courts (here, the Florida Supreme Court) the power under §102.168(8) to "provide any relief appropriate under [the] circumstances." If Gore won the statewide recount ordered under the authority of §102.168(8) by the Florida Supreme Court on December 8, 2000, his victory was, under 3 U.S.C. §15, "supported by the decision of such state as authorized by *its* law." In other words,

(cont. p. 158)

Amendment even specifically provides for what Congress should do when neither side has a majority of electors.) Indeed, even the regents of rubbish who make the argument about the Supreme Court avoiding a constitutional crisis concede that the determination of which electoral votes to count is supposed to take place in Congress. But they, in effect, say that to avoid this possible dispute in Congress (they call it a "crisis," I imagine to conjure up in the minds of their audience images of the nation being paralyzed, and the planes and trains, if they run at all, certainly no longer running on time), the Supreme Court, just willy-nilly, should take the matter away from Congress and they, not Congress, should resolve the problem. But in a close, contested election, there's no more authority for the Supreme Court to pick the president than for the Des Moines Rotary Club or Boston Symphony to do so. If anyone tells you there is such authority, what is it? What statute, what case, what rule or regulation, what historical precedent? There is, of course, no authority. There is nothing at all.

Congress is set up to handle all types of intensely contested and combustible issues. And the law of the land is that the determination of who got the most valid electoral votes in a presidential election is one of them. The Supreme Court has no such lawful authority. Yet the pharoahs of farce, who believe in very strictly following the law about vote dead-

---

3 U.S.C. §15, which is a *federal* statute passed by Congress pursuant to the 12th Amendment, says that *Florida's* law is dispositive on the issue of which electors Congress should choose. Here, not only would Gore's electors have the imprimatur of the Florida Supreme Court acting under Florida law, but §103.011 of the Florida Election Code, a Florida law that curiously was rarely mentioned in the election debate, expressly provides that in a general election, "Votes cast for the actual candidates for President and Vice President shall be counted as votes cast for the presidential electors supporting such candidates. The Department of State shall certify as elected the presidential electors of the candidates for President and Vice President *who receive the highest number of votes.*" In any event, it would be up to Congress to resolve the dispute. This is what the United States Constitution directs under the twelveth Amendment, and the U.S. Supreme Court had no authority whatsoever to usurp this constitutional right that Congress had.

lines—a second past the deadline won't do, just ask Katherine Harris—have no trouble at all advocating that the Supreme Court literally usurp the constitutional authority of Congress to determine who received the most valid electoral votes for president in a close election. And they are so unhinged and crazy (all traceable to their partisanship, of course) that they don't even care if there's any true, legitimate dispute in Congress to resolve. It doesn't matter if the dispute is contrived and illegitimate because it is caused by a rogue, partisan and extremely unprincipled Florida legislature which was threatening to give Florida to Bush even if Gore ended up winning the popular vote. So in any close presidential race in the future, any state legislature controlled by a political party which knows it has a majority of the same party on the Supreme Court who they feel will be as audacious and unprincipled as they are, can intentionally create a "crisis" by threatening to send in electors who do not represent the will of the people of their state, and then let their friends on the Supreme Court take over from there. I see.

The notion that any legislative body or any governing or executive commission, committee, or association (e.g., a state corporation commission, a real estate board, the National Baskestball Association, etc.) entrusted with the responsibility of resolving disputes among its members can only do so if the disputes are easy to handle, and if not, some other entity, without any authority at all, can simply take over and send the established body on its way, is so far outside our human experience and so absurd that it should not be the subject of any discussion. That is, but for what the U.S. Supreme Court did in *Bush v. Gore*, and the stratospheric hubris of the Court.

The Court, through the years, has incrementally extended its tentacles and influence over every area of American life. In wearing out several mirrors admiring the limitless power it has arrogated to itself, it apparently now feels it can do anything at all—even engage in seriously criminal behavior. As envisioned by the framers of the Constitution, the three branches of government (legislative, executive, and judicial) established in Articles 1, 2, and 3 of the U.S. Constitution were supposed to be coequal branches. But there can be no question that the judicial branch has become first among equals, making it preeminent in the constitutional constellation.

Going back to section 3 U.S.C. 5, one thing is very clear about the safe harbor provision of that statute, and that is that the harbor is shrouded in a fog that, together with loose language by the Florida Supreme Court and an unfortunate concession by Gore's chief trial lawyer, David Boies, enabled the U.S. Supreme Court to treat December 12 like something it wasn't, a deadline to count votes.

It must be noted off the top that not only, by its very language, is 3 U.S.C. §5 not a *federal* deadline of December 12 for the counting of votes in a presidential election, but there is no state statute in Florida providing for December 12 being the cutoff date for the counting of votes. To illustrate the lack of certitude by the parties in the Florida election dispute over just what the December 12 date means, in oral argument before the Florida Supreme Court on November 20, Chief Justice Charles J. Wells, who, in his long and discursive questions during oral argument made Eisenhower's syntax look positively Churchillian, was wondering out loud whether or not the controversy then extant in the election would have to be determined by December 12. In other words, he wasn't sure—to the point where he felt impelled to ask (not tell) Boies "do you agree" that December 12 was the deadline? There should have been only one answer from Boies (who at that early point may not have known that December 12 was merely a date where, if electors were chosen by then, their legitimacy would be immunized from being challenged in Congress), and that was, "Your honor, the only deadline there should obviously be in this case is when all the votes are counted." Instead, he improvidently answered, "I do, your honor."

That unfortunate and unnecessary concession from Gore's own lawyer may at least have been partially responsible for the Florida Supreme Court, in just one sentence of its 50 page opinion on Decmeber 8, saying that they considered the Florida election statutes to be *"cognizant* of the federal grant of authority derived from the United States Constitution *and derived from* 3 U.S.C. §5 . . ." But they never said nor even implied how they reached that conclusion. I mean, did they get a telephone call or a letter from the Florida legislature saying that the Florida election statutes they enacted were enacted by them with 3 U.S.C. §5 in mind? It may just have been loose language on the court's part, because in the very next paragraph, they said: "This case today is *controlled* by the language set forth by the legislature in section 102.158, Florida Statutes."

Despite the fact that the overwhelming weight and thrust of the Florida Supreme Court's two long opinions was that they wanted to insure that the will of the people of the state not be subordinated to hypertechnical statutory deadlines and that all valid votes be counted, and further, that the statutory scheme enacted by the Florida legislature was consistent with this, the one word "cognizant" that the court used in its December 8 opinion, plus a reference by the court in a footnote of the same opinion to "looming deadlines" was apparently enough, per L. Kinvin Wroth, dean of the Vermont Law School, for the U.S. Supreme Court majority to "play gotcha," go on to actually say in their opinion that "the Florida Supreme Court has said that the Florida legislature intended to obtain the safe harbor benefits of 3 U.S.C. §5," and treat December 12 as a deadline for the counting of votes.

The reason why the U.S. Supreme Court's assumption that the Florida Supreme Court believed that the Florida legislature wanted to avail themselves of the safe harbor protection under 3 U.S.C. §5 is tenuous at best is that the Florida Supreme Court, in turn, would have had to make the assumption that it was more important to the Florida legislature that they obtain safe harbor protection for their electors than to continue the recount and find out who really won the election in their state. Although this particular Florida legislature, being strongly, almost militantly pro-Bush, gave every indication that they wanted to convene a special session and name 25 electors for Bush, even if it turned out he lost, the justices on the Florida Supreme Court clearly were thinking in a high-minded, principled way when they wrote their opinion.

A point that cannot be overlooked, though it is so easy to do so, is that even with the U.S. Supreme Court's reliance on a hypertechnical, abstruse, and very obscure federal statutory provision to thwart the will of the American people, if they hadn't improperly stopped the recount on December 9, which was scheduled to be completed the next day at 5:00 P.M., even the alleged "deadline" date of December 12 under 3 U.S.C. §5 *would* have been complied with, and *no one* would have been able to complain.

NOTE THREE

THE BUSH TEAM of lawyers called far more witnesses than Gore's lawyers did, but one Bush witness "made every point we were trying to make," David Boies, Gore's chief trial lawyer, said. John Ahman, who in the 1960s helped design the Votomatic punch card system still in use in Florida, strongly defended the accuracy and efficiency of the Votomatic machines on direct examination. But on cross-examination by Gore lawyer Stephen Zack, Zack read aloud Ahman's own words in a patent application of Ahman's where he was seeking a patent on a new Votomatic machine because the old ones could become so clogged up with chads that "serious errors" could occur. Zack noted that Miami-Dade County last cleaned the chads from their Votomatic machines eight years ago. More importantly, Ahman conceded on cross that it "is advisable" in "very close elections" to have a manual recount to determine the voter's intent.

NOTE FOUR

OF COURSE, THE duty of a trial lawyer is never to assume that the judge knows the law of a case. Any experienced trial lawyer will tell you this. Always, without exception, a trial lawyer has to inform the judge what he perceives to be the law applicable to the case. Particularly in a situation like this, where Sauls, during the two day hearing, gave no indication that he was a legal or mental giant, Gore's lawyer, David Boies, should have put a bib on Sauls and spoon-fed him. But he did not. Instead of starting out his argument by stating very clearly what his burden of proof was under §102.168 of the Florida Election Code, and, indeed, reading the exact language of the statute to Sauls, then proceeding to argue to Sauls why he believed he met this burden, and then *at least* one more time, near the end of his summation, repeating and reemphasizing what his legal burden was, and that he had met it, remarkably, Boies did neither. Instead, his only very brief, passing reference (one that presumed Sauls already knew the law) was at the tail end of a sentence buried in the middle of his oral argument: "If you have," Boies said, "only a fraction of one percent of ballots from which you can discern the voter's intent, but the machine cannot read, those ballots are sufficient to change the result of the election and certainly to place that result in doubt, the standard of a 168 contest action." Not only do we know that this almost parenthetical observation by Boies went over Sauls' head without his even feeling the breeze, but Boies only referred to "the standard," not his "burden of proof," a term trial lawyers and courts all use.

The reality is that, legally speaking, Sauls did not know what the hell was going on in his courtroom, and Boies did virtually nothing to help Sauls end his blissfully benighted state. It has to be added that if Boies had properly argued the burden of proof issue, at the core of all cases, civil and criminal, Sauls would simply have not been able to utter the words he did in his order. He may have ruled the same way, but he would not, could not, have used the words he did.

BIOGRAPHY

VINCENT BUGLIOSI RECEIVED his law degree in 1964 from U.C.L.A. law school, where he was president of his graduating class. In his career as a prosecutor for the Los Angeles County District Attorney's office, he successfully prosecuted 105 out of 106 felony jury trials, including twenty-one murder convictions without a single loss. His most famous trial was the Charles Manson case, which became the basis of his true crime classic, *Helter Skelter*, the biggest selling true crime book in publishing history. But even before the Manson case, in the television series *The DA*, actor Robert Conrad patterned his starring role after Bugliosi.

Bugliosi has uncommonly attained success in two separate and distinct fields, as a lawyer and an author. Three of his true crime books, *Helter Skelter*, *And The Sea Will Tell*, and *Outrage, The Five Reasons Why O.J. Simpson Got Away With Murder*, reached number one on the *New York Times* hardcover bestseller list. No other American true crime author has ever had more than one book that achieved this ranking.

And as a trial lawyer, the judgment of his peers says it all. "Bugliosi is as good a prosecutor as there ever was," Alan Dershowitz says. F. Lee Bailey calls Bugliosi "the quintessential prosecutor." Harry Weiss, a veteran criminal defense attorney who has gone up against Bugliosi in court, says: "I've seen all the great trial lawyers of the past thirty years and none of them are in Vince's class." Robert Tanenbaum, for years the top prosecutor in the Manhattan District Attorney's office, says, "There is only one Vince Bugliosi. He's the best." Perhaps most telling of all is the comment by Gerry Spence, who squared off against Bugliosi in a twenty-one hour televised, scriptless "docutrial" of Lee Harvey Oswald, in which the original key witnesses to the Kennedy assassination testified and were cross-examined. After the Dallas jury returned a guilty verdict in Bugliosi's favor, Spence said, "No other lawyer in America could have done what Vince did in this case."

With the recent compilation CD he produced, *Greatest Latin Love Songs Of The Century*, which the incomparable Chilean, Lucho Gatica—whom many believe to be the greatest singer of boleros Latin America has ever produced— calls "the best album of Latin love songs I have ever heard," Bugliosi seems to be launching yet another career.

Bugliosi lives with his wife in Los Angeles and is working on a book about the assassination of President John F. Kennedy.